*Through the Jungle of Death*

# Through the Jungle of Death

## A Boy's Escape from Wartime Burma

### STEPHEN BROOKES

John Wiley & Sons, Inc.

*New York • Chichester • Weinheim • Brisbane • Singapore • Toronto*

Published by John Wiley & Sons, Inc.

Published by arrangement with John Murray (Publishers) Ltd.

This publication is designed to provide accurate and authoritative information in regard to the subject matter covered. It is sold with the understanding that the publisher is not engaged in rendering professional services. If professional advice or other expert assistance is required, the services of a competent professional person should be sought.

Library of Congress Cataloging-in-Publication Data

Brookes, Stephen.
    Through the jungle of death : a boy's wartime escape from Burma / Stephen Brookes.
        p. cm.
    ISBN 0-471-41569-3 (cloth : alk. paper)
    1. Brookes, Stephen.   2. World War, 1939–1945—Personal narratives, Burmese.   3. World War, 1939–1945—Burma.   4. Boys—Burma—Biography.   5. Brooks family.   I. Title.

D811.5 .B7553 2001
940.54'81591–dc21

                                                        2001017666

Printed in the United States of America

10 9 8 7 6 5 4 3 2 1

# Contents

# Contents

# Illustrations

*In memory of my family*
*who trekked through the Valley of Death with me:*
*Ma Sein, William Lindfield Brookes,*
*Maisie and George*

ROUTE OF THE BROOKES FAMILY, 1942
Miles 0 50 100 150 200
0 80 160 240 320 Kms.
TIBET
CHINA
INDIA
Pangsau Pass
R. Brahmaputra
Margherita
Hukawng Valley
To Calcutta
Shingbwiyang
Sumprabum
Gauhati
milepost 102
Pandu
Patkoi Range
Maingkwan
Kumon Range
REMAINS OF CHINESE FIFTH ARMY
R. Chindwin
Myitkyina
BURMA
Mangshih
Tamu
Katha
Bhamo
R. Irrawaddy
Namkham
Kutkai
Hsenwi
Kalewa
Lashio
BRITISH ARMY AND EVACUEES
JAPANESE ARMY
PART OF CHINESE FIFTH, SIXTH ARMY
Maymyo (START)
Mandalay
JAPANESE ARMY
Peking
CHINA
Delhi
Nanking
INDIA
Calcutta
Hong Kong
AREA OF MAIN MAP
AUSTRALIA

*Each day the petals fall*
*But the fragrance lingers,*
*Filling the imagination*
*With eternal memories.*

# Prologue

In a little-known corner of Asia there was once a land as fair as any that a traveller could hope to discover. It is still there, though you would have difficulty in relating what you see now to the splendour of how things used to be before the armies of Japan, Britain and China fought over it for four years and left it broken and brutalised.

This is the country that Marco Polo and the Mongols of Kublai Khan named the Kingdom of Mien, which the British knew as Burma and which is now also called Myanmar. Once, in the springtime of its history, its kings built an eloquent capital called Pagan which was studded with over 4,000 pagodas scattered over fifteen square miles in a loop of the Irrawaddy river. Gold, silver, glazed tiles, murals and sculptures adorned the magnificent buildings. In 1287, about the same time as Edward I of England was trying to assert his will over Scotland and Wales, a Mongol army entered Burma through its border with China and destroyed Pagan. The blow destabilised the country, plunging it into anarchy for 300 years before it was reunited under strong and warlike rulers.

Early in the nineteenth century the British began to exert their influence over the Burmese king and his court. In the ensuing conflict the Burmese were defeated and the country was annexed in 1886. King Thibaw and his consort Queen Supayalat were removed from their palace in Mandalay in a simple bullock cart and banished to India for life. Thibaw spent thirty unhappy years in exile until his death in 1916, after which Supayalat was allowed to return to Burma where she died in anonymity.

Yet they found immortality of a sort in the Victorian music-halls, where the British audiences revelled in singing the words of Kipling's nostalgic 'Mandalay':

'Er petticoat was yaller an' 'er little cap was green,
An' 'er name was Supi-yaw-lat jes' the same as Theebaw's Queen,
An' I seed her first a-smokin' of a whackin' white cheroot,
An' a-wastin' Christian kisses on an 'eathen idol's foot . . .
    On the road to Mandalay,
    Where the flyin'-fishes play,
    An' the dawn comes up like thunder outer China
      'crost the Bay!

In the days before the Second World War there were no all-weather metalled roads leading over the mountain barriers that separated Burma from her neighbours India, Tibet and China. However there were jungle tracks which traders had used for centuries leading to Assam and Thailand, besides the route to China that the Mongols had used 655 years before. It was the highway built along this route to carry Allied war supplies to China that became known to modern history in 1942 as the 'Burma Road'.

These tracks crossed formidable terrain where landslides were common, especially during the monsoon season when torrents of water poured down the hill slopes, transforming the tiniest brook into a dangerous obstacle. Rickety suspension bridges spanned some of the gorges while bamboo pontoons on wired pulleys provided a perilous crossing of the open sections. Since the whole northern territory was a fertile breeding-ground for virulent forms of tropical diseases it is hardly surprising that, with the exception of political officers, government officials, and intrepid plant-hunters like Frank Kingdon-Ward, few foreigners used these trails.

The country, roughly the combined area of England and France, was rich in natural resources including petroleum, which was exploited by the Burmah Oil Company in 1889 long before many of the oil-fields in the Middle East were developed. Ample teak and hardwoods grew in the forests and in the ground were deposits of silver, lead, tungsten, sapphires, rubies and jade. Before the Second World War rice was grown in such abundance that Burma became the largest exporter of rice in the world.

The bulk of these products were transported by the old Irrawaddy Flotilla Company which managed one of the largest fleet of ferries, barges and steamers in Asia. Their main highway was the placid Irrawaddy river which was navigable for almost one thousand miles.

Burma was truly a green and pleasant land and its people, too, were pleasant and friendly. Unlike the Indians to the west or the Chinese to the east with their huge populations and harsh landscape, the Burmese shared much of the same culture and relaxed attitude to life as the Khmers and Mons of Thailand and Cambodia.

Tragically this peaceful scene was not to last, for on the morning of Sunday, 7 December 1941, 360 aircraft from an undetected Japanese naval force bombed the American Pacific Fleet at anchor in the naval base at Pearl Harbor in Hawaii, causing substantial damage. America and Britain responded by declaring war on Japan.

The next day Japanese planes bombed Singapore, Hong Kong, Malaya and the Philippines. But the severest threat to the British forces in Asia came on 10 December 1941 when the battleships HMS Repulse and HMS Prince of Wales were sunk by Japanese aircraft off the coast of Malaya while they were attempting to intercept an enemy seaborne landing. At a stroke Burma, Malaya and Singapore were exposed. By 27 January 1942 Malaya had fallen to the Japanese. Less than three weeks later the British garrison in Singapore surrendered.

On 23 December and again on Christmas Day the Burmese capital Rangoon was bombed. By 18 January 1942 the Japanese had entered the country in strength. The following day the town of Tavoy, just three hundred miles from the capital was taken. Burma's long agony had begun.

During their thousand-mile retreat the British adopted a scorched-earth policy to delay the Japanese. Anything of use was destroyed: the docks, storage depots, railways, bridges including the huge Ava bridge across the Irrawaddy near Mandalay, airfields, roads, the oil-fields at Yenangyaung and the refineries at Syriam. Rangoon disappeared under a pall of black smoke and flames and 600 ships of the Irrawaddy Flotilla Company were scuttled. Even the palace of King Thibaw at Fort Dufferin in Mandalay was destroyed when they returned four years later.

Meanwhile the Japanese bombed and burned what remained standing, using incendiary devices to destroy the wooden homes of civilians in towns such as Mandalay. The Burmese people endured the destruction of their homeland from 1941 to 1945 during the longest unbroken campaign fought by the British in the Second World War. In the event, it was here that the Japanese suffered the greatest defeat on land that their forces had ever known.

As early as December 1941, when Rangoon was bombed, the Indian workers in the docks and the municipal services tried to escape to India via the Taungup pass. They were prevented from leaving their posts by the Burma Government which cynically ordered the closure of this escape route. However when the Japanese broke through the British forces defending the capital they joined the general stampede to safety. Between 100,000 and 200,000 Indians eventually reached India via this route. Large numbers died on the way and according to one report their casualties were greater than those on the other escape routes. Meanwhile the Government of Burma departed to the safety of Maymyo in the north and ceased to have any influence on the administration or organisation of the country.

At this point the Japanese swung northwards driving a vast horde of terrified refugees before them. These headed for the next exit to India via the tracks through the towns of Kalewa and Tamu, but their hopes of escape were extinguished when the Indian Government issued orders limiting the flow to 500 per day.

Like a herd of cattle, 100,000 were diverted to Mandalay where the Japanese bombers found them on Good Friday 1942. Many were killed and the rest scattered into the countryside. Those who remained in the refugee camps were dying at the rate of 500 per day from cholera. The officials who had worked tirelessly to assist and organise the evacuation of the refugees wrote critical reports of the Government of Burma but, ominously, the most telling of these appears to have been suppressed.

As the situation worsened civilians were permitted to use the road to Tamu which had been built by the army. By the end of April the British army was in full retreat and orders were issued to receive troops instead of civilians. The priority for food and transport was switched away from them immediately; but by the middle of May, when the army was safely in India, civilians were allowed back on the road. By the end of July approximately 150,000 to 200,000 refugees had passed through to India.

About 50,000 refugees were swept even further northwards. Many died of disease and starvation in the jungle and swamps of the Kumon range, the Hukawng Valley, Mogaung and Sumprabum. But the torment of those who were still alive was to last for a further five months until October, because the escape route was closed at the village of Shingbwiyang by Major-General Wood, the Administrator General.

The officer responsible for the air-dropping of supplies

estimated that 45,000 refugees and Chinese soldiers arrived at this village. Yet the Indian Tea Association, a group of Indian teaplanters and their employees who organised the relief effort until July, accounted for only 20,344 on the Indian border. Allowing for errors and the few who managed to survive the monsoon in villages along the way, it is clear from these figures that a huge number died at Shingbwiyang because of this decision.

At about this time a conference of the relief organisations responsible for assistance along this route was informed that although New Delhi was making arrangements to feed the refugees at Shingbwiyang by dropping supplies by air, 'it may be necessary, for reasons of a confidential nature, to investigate the possibility of further reducing the numbers left at that ill-fated place.'

What deceit lies behind those words? Was someone already aware that preparations at Shingbwiyang were so inadequate that large numbers of evacuees were about to die? What cynicism underlies the phrase 'for reasons of a confidential nature'?

The scale of the débâcle over the evacuation of civilians is clear from a Government of India estimate that between 450,000 and 500,000 'British Asiatics' arrived in India from Burma. They had lost everything, not just money and property, but their families and friends. Estimates of the dead range from 50,000 to 100,000.

By comparison, the casualties of General Slim's army in Burma during the same period in 1942 amounted to 13,000 men killed, wounded or missing. The Japanese lost only 4,600 men killed and wounded.

My own family was among those 50,000 refugees who

fled northwards to India via Shingbwiyang and the terrible swamps and jungle of the Hukawng Valley. My childhood memory of the trek through that valley, also known as the Valley of Death, has haunted me for more than fifty years.

# I   *Soldiers of the King*

The men who ruled the British Empire when I was a boy had an obsessive liking for military parades. They treated us to these archaic martial spectacles with tedious regularity because Maymyo, the town to the north of Rangoon where my family lived, was a garrison station. On the King's Birthday, Armistice Day, Jubilee Day, Empire Day and a dozen other suitable days, long columns of armed troops would emerge from their barracks, rifles and bayonets bobbing above the leafy hedgerows as they marched about like so many giant hairy caterpillars.

Since all the men in my family were in the army, my sisters and I would often go down to wave at them as they marched and countermarched on the dusty parade-ground. Row upon row of soldiers in columns of three ranks, uniforms sharp with starch, polished buckles twinkling on green webbing. Their ankles were wrapped with puttees and on their heads were forage caps or broad-brimmed bush hats or pith helmets sporting the large green pompom of the King's Own Yorkshire Light Infantry.

We knew several KOYLI soldiers since my father used to invite them to our home for dinner or Sunday lunch, feeling sorry for these men who were so far from their homes in England. But I remember these troops for another reason – it is the catchy marching tune their rumbustious brass band played with such panache that still evokes the unique mood and quality of those precious peacetime years. Almost sixty years on, I need only whistle it and the child comes alive, clear-eyed, in his sister's arms, head thrown back in ecstasy at the tumult of the band, cheering the rows of marching soldiers.

Maymyo was a pretty hill station, 3,500 feet up on a plateau in central Burma, where retired military and government officers spent their last days in peace and elegance, soothed by a pleasantly temperate climate. Their bungalows and the picturesque gardens surrounding them reproduced in every detail the cottage gardens of England at the turn of the century. Even nature was harnessed to the cause of nostalgia with the construction of rides through the forest, a Botanical Garden with lakes, and exclusive golf, polo and tennis clubs. And to complement these reminders of 'home', Maymo was famous for growing in lavish abundance the tastiest strawberries in the land. With attractions such as these, it was no wonder to us that the Government of Burma chose Maymo as their retreat from Rangoon during the hot summer months.

At the edge of the town was a tree-lined avenue called Fryer Road, so quiet you could almost hear the grass grow on lazy Sunday afternoons. About halfway along and set back behind a row of cherry trees and a tall, well-manicured privet hedge, was a four-acre plot of land on which stood a large rambling house with wide airy verandahs and floors of glowing polished teak. I thought this place was Paradise when I was little but I discovered much later that it was called 'Lindfield', the house where I was born.

There were tiger and leopard skins on the drawing-room floor and elephant tusks in one corner near the organ which my sister Maisie played. Close by were display cabinets with gold, silver, jade and ivory ornaments and jars full of rubies, while on the wall hung a superb oil portrait of my Burmese mother next to a similar painting of my father's Scottish mother, Granny Stuart. At the eastern end of the drawing-room were bedrooms which led to my father's medical surgery and library, while to the west were his gunroom and more bedrooms. To the rear of the building was the dining-room, with its huge teak table at which my parents, their eight children, guests and occasionally my three half-sisters, consumed a prodigious quantity of delicious food prepared by Ohn Sein, our neurotic cook.

Around the house, land was set aside for rows of sweet-corn and potatoes, a well-stocked kitchen garden, extensive orchards, lawns and a number of formal gardens sheltered by oak and eucalyptus trees. Beyond the porch, where my mother's favourite orchids hung in extravagant clusters, was the parking area for the Oldsmobile convertible. From here a track led to the dog kennels, coops for chickens and geese, and a pleasant row of quarters for the servants.

I was the last of eleven children who made up the Brookes family, an affectionate boy with an overactive and intensely inquisitive mind. By the time I was old enough to be aware of who I was, most of the older siblings had married and left home, but we met occasionally when war was declared and Lindfield became the focal point for the families of the men on the front line.

My father, Major William Lindfield Brookes, had spent his entire working life in the Indian army. He had the constitution of a man of 50, looked like someone of 60 – but was actually a few weeks short of his seventieth birthday in 1942. He had retired in 1927 but rejoined the army in 1941 at the outbreak of war with Japan.

Born in India, he had qualified as a surgeon and first saw action in 1897 as a 25-year-old Assistant Surgeon during the campaign in the Tirah in the North-West Frontier Province of Afghanistan. I have a vague childhood memory that he was also in Mesopotamia around the time of the First World War. Most of his medals appear to have vanished mysteriously but I have two: the India Medal 1895 with bars for the Punjab Frontier 1897–8 and the Tirah 1897–8; and the British War Medal 1914–18.

Family legend relates that soon after his posting to Burma, while he was learning the Burmese language, he fell in love with his teacher's exquisite young daughter and decided to marry her as soon as he had finished his course. She was only 16, her name was Ma Sein – Miss Diamond – and she could speak no English. He was a 38-year-old widower with three little daughters under the age of 10. The year was 1910 and they were married in Kindat, Upper Chindwin, by the Rev. Chapman, General Superintendent of the Methodist Mission.

From then on Father's career in the army was blighted, yet he and Ma Sein flourished for thirty-two years in singular warmth and harmony. She bore him four girls and four boys – and I revelled in being the youngest.

As to the slights and prejudices of the small-minded, they were of little consequence to my parents for they were confident in themselves and in their love and admiration for one another. When an invitation to an official function was addressed to 'Major Brookes' only and not 'Major and Mrs Brookes', my father's response was to burst into the Government Secretary's office like a wild bull and frighten the man out of his wits. He left through the closed French windows, leaving behind shattered glass and a shaken secretary. He was my kind of man, fearless and resolute, with no mealy-mouthed 'ifs' or 'buts' or 'maybes' in his vocabulary. His army papers include the adverse comment that he was 'ordered to proceed to Yeravada but refused to go'. How like my Old Man to have the courage to live life on his own terms.

His name for my mother was Puss. Far from being a timid handmaid, she was his equal in boldness and determination, standing up to him when others would have tactfully given way. She ran the household at Lindfield, both family and servants, like a queen dealing with matters of state. And on Sundays, or when important guests were present, she would indeed dress like a queen, radiant in gold and jewels and smelling of fresh sandalwood. Her shimmering Thai silk longyi was edged with threads of gold; gold buttons held her blouse of purest white, and jewelled rings, bracelets, hair-grips and necklaces completed her adornments. My favourite task was to thread a garland of white jasmine flowers for her to wind round the tall bun on her head in the traditional Burmese fashion.

I could not have had a more fascinating couple for parents. The age-gap of fifty-eight years between my father and myself seemed to enhance rather than obstruct our relationship, much to the amusement and envy of family and friends. He taught me to play chess when I was 10 and glowed with pleasure when I demolished adult guests who dared to challenge me. I was the only one allowed to sit in his surgery and experiment with chemicals – except for poisons, which he kept out of my reach on the top shelf in case curiosity overcame prudence. However I must confess that on two occasions I did offer my brother George some chocolates dipped in substances from bottles clearly marked with a skull and crossbones. Yet apart from a touch of diarrhoea, which he shrugged off, George remained surprisingly frisky.

Father and I shared the joy of books and the pleasure of singing: his wistful rendering of 'Macushla' echoed in my 'Rose of Tralee'. He encouraged me to cook and I remember the alarm on the faces of my brothers and sisters when he insisted that everyone had to eat my offerings, even the sparrow curry. The wild jungle enchanted us both, and I trusted him when he taught me how to hold a live poisonous snake in my bare hand, even though the exposed fangs and the writhing body wrapped around my small forearm made me shiver with fear.

Despite his martial exterior, Father was a very religious man, a lay preacher in the Baptist Church with an Abraham-like presence, who was capable of calling down fire and brimstone on the congregation. Meanwhile my sister Maisie soothed their ruffled nerves by playing the organ, my brother Richard taught in the Sunday School, my brother-in-law Dennis was a Deacon, and at Christmas George and I were two of the three kings of a place called Orien-Tar.

Even so, I was fortunate to have the moderating influence of my mother to soften the hard edges of the male Brookes. She was the embodiment of the tactile Asian mother, her arms for ever open to comfort and restore a grieving child. Through her I learnt to heed the oneness of all life in the exuberant forms around me. From her I learnt to be mindful of the spirits, or nats, who were the invisible forces of good and evil. These spirits occasionally appeared at night as globes of light, drifting silently through the branches of the banyan tree at the bottom of the garden. Richard, always practical and scornful of such bizarre ideas, dismissed the lights as fireflies. Even so, I still held my palms together as Mum had taught me, to signify to the lights 'I see the God in you' – just to be on the safe side.

In our corner of Maymyo, bordering Fryer Road, Nestwood Hill and Circular Road, were properties similar to our own and in them lived our friends with British names like Langtry, Plunket, Fenton, Jellico, O'Hara, Lovett, Vincent, Edwards and Russell. My older sisters and brothers grew up with them, went to the same schools and attended the same social and sporting events. Despite the passing of over half a century, I am in contact with many of them still.

And so I played, heedless of the passing years, unaware that the sun was finally setting on the once great British Empire. My days were brim-full of wonders. My universe at Lindfield was filled with relatives, friends and servants, sometimes as many as eighteen people, scattered around the living quarters and gardens. All of them were older than I was, yet I was never short of company or affection. And from them, Asian and European alike, I absorbed the insight and fortitude that would be the foundation of my survival when the black days of adversity came.

## 2 *Bombers over Paradise*

By the autumn of 1941 all the men in my family had gone to war, leaving my brother George and me to guard the homestead. He was 14 and I was 11. By any reckoning the obligation to defend four acres of tropical gardens, orchards and ancient oaks at Lindfield was a heavy one. But we were at that brief, beguiling stage in life when reality and fantasy merged. In our world no one really died in combat and all wars stopped at supper time.

Ignorant of the worsening situation at the front line, my brother and I went to sleep each night with our Daisy air-guns tucked under our beds, confident that we would stop the rot when duty called, and quite untroubled by the knowledge that our rusty weapons regularly missed targets two feet wide and twelve feet away. We knew nothing of the flying machine called an aeroplane, for we had never seen one in our remote corner of the Empire, had never experienced the terror of exploding bombs, or heard the crisp rattle of machine-gun fire. All we knew was that we would stand and fight when the call to arms was sounded.

How could I know that the grim reality of war made nonsense of my foolish fancies? Even as George and I played with our dogs Socksie and Blackie in the fading twilight, time was running out for this Eden. Within a few weeks of the departure of our men the full-scale invasion of Burma by the Japanese army began.

Two days before Christmas, Rangoon was in flames and 4,450 people had been killed or wounded by Japanese bombing. To the east, the Japanese poured out of the jungles on the Thai border, causing confusion at all levels of the defending British forces. It was clear that a catastrophe was about to overtake the civilian population yet the Government, headed by Sir Reginald Dorman-Smith, did everything in its power to prevent them from leaving when they had the time and opportunity to do so.

As the Japanese closed in, orders were issued for the destruction of Rangoon. Tragically the gates of the prison and the mental asylum were thrown open, releasing the bemused inmates to wander aimlessly through the burning city with no one to care for them, since their warders had fled. It was into this madhouse that the Japanese marched on 8 March 1942.

The enemy now swung northwards on a broad front, driving the British army, two Chinese armies and a horde of terrified civilians before them. By the beginning of April they were less than 200 miles from us and moving fast. The impotent Government, now based at Maymyo, had ceased to play any part in the administration of the country and the civilian population was abandoned to its fate. The lucky few escaped immediately by air and sea. But for the great majority of the refugees, who set out on foot through the jungles to India via Taungup, Kalewa, Tamu and the Hukawng Valley, the escape was a nightmare.

There was not a moment to lose if we were to get our own family away to safety, which should have been a fairly simple matter since all the men were in the army. My married sisters Louise, Janet, Marie, my half-sister Dorothy and their children were flown from various parts of Burma to India in military planes, while my half-sister Kate set out on foot. However, my mother, my half-sister Queenie and my sister-in-law Della decided, for reasons of their own, to delay their departure and that of their children. By this single act they unwittingly altered the whole direction of our future.

Meantime at Lindfield we were scarcely aware of outside events since war was beginning to disrupt communications; indeed, with only Mum, Maisie, George and me in residence, the house had an unusually peaceful air. Sometime during the first week of April a visitor came to see Mum and while they talked in the lounge I sat on the step by the back door cleaning my Daisy air-rifle and dreaming of better days. Then, quite suddenly, the world fell apart.

An unnatural, high-pitched screech, full of terror and indescribable pain rang through the empty spaces of our home. It came again and again, growing wilder, like the sound of a crazed animal in agony. The effect on me was so violent that I seemed to lose my ability to think clearly. Then I heard a voice.

'No ... No ... No ... Please God ... No ...'

It was my mother – but I could not move. I should have gone to her, but fear of the unknown horror that had distressed her crushed my will. The moment for my gallant intervention had arrived, but the challenge was too fearful for a rational response.

She screamed again: 'Please God, not Richard ... Please God, not Richard. Richard, my son ... Richard ... Richard ... my son ... my son ...'

This was no Anglo-Saxon lady discreetly weeping into a folded handkerchief. This was an Asian woman, distraught, broken, tearing at her clothes and hair in uncontrollable grief. I guessed what news the visitor had brought from the intensity of her pain: Richard had been killed.

Mum needed me now as never before, but in a burst of irresponsibility I ran away. Unable to cope with my rising panic I fled as if possessed to the far corner of Lindfield, to the eucalyptus tree on which we children carved our names. Through my tears I found the one I was looking for: RICHARD. I hugged the tree as though my life depended on it, for it was my only hold on something solid as my head seethed and my stomach churned.

I echoed my mother's plea: 'Please God, not Dickie. Not Dickie, please.' But a hideous feeling of finality sent a shiver down my back. Time passed, yet it seemed that I would never be able to stop weeping. Finally, about an hour later, I stumbled back to the silent house where I found the door to my parents' bedroom shut. Mum was alone: I had failed her.

For the next few days an impenetrable gloom, such as I had never encountered before, hung over Lindfield. My mother was inconsolable. She lay on her bed under a pile of quilts, eating and saying nothing. The only sounds that came from the bedroom were heartrending groans and sobs which went on hour after hour. After three days I thought she was going to die.

It was almost impossible to take in the bad news. The official report described how, on 4 April 1942, Richard was in a supply column near the battle front at Allanmyo when it was attacked by Japanese planes. In the chaos that followed the trucks halted and the men dispersed, but before my brother could reach safety he was badly wounded. After the raid was over the other soldiers emerged from their shelters and carried Richard back to a truck; but as the truck started off down the road the planes returned to the attack. The others ran for cover leaving my brother in the truck. It received a direct hit from a bomb which killed him instantly.

Unlike the 'hunting/shooting' males in my family, Richard – who was in his early twenties – was a gentle, kindly person who might have become a teacher or perhaps a missionary had he lived. Like other young volunteers in the two World Wars, he joined up because it was a duty, something that was expected of him by his peers. Like many of them, he paid the price in full, leaving a gap in our lives that was never filled.

Things now took a further alarming turn when Queenie, Della and their children arrived unannounced at Lindfield, having decided to wait there for their husbands rather than escape with the others by military aircraft. I was too young and confused by events to appreciate the full gravity of this decision, yet even I had an uneasy feeling that the confusion of war would make nonsense of this move.

Almost simultaneously we lost contact with Father, who was stationed in Mandalay as officer-in-charge of the Medical Supply Depot at Fort Dufferin. The day after my sisters' arrival news came that Mandalay, only 42 miles away, had been heavily bombed on 3 April, the day before Richard was killed. Entire districts had been burnt to the ground, the station, hospital and other essential services destroyed and hundreds had perished in the flames. The bombers returned over the next few days until nothing remained of the town except acres of ash and smouldering ruins. Mandalay, the ancient capital of King Thibaw, ceased to exist.

We heard a few days later that Father was safe and desperately trying to cope with the problem of treating the dying, disposing of the dead, and stopping the spread of cholera. The situation was almost out of control because 100,000 refugees from Rangoon were camped at Mandalay, due to the refusal of the civil and military authorities to let them use the track to India. After the bombing these unfortunate people, who had been dying of cholera at the rate of 500 each day, scattered in panic.

The past few days had been filled with such doom and disaster we almost believed this must be the end of it. Looking forward to a little peace, George and I dozed contentedly, after a heavy lunch, in the branches of a cherry tree. It was one of six, each over twenty feet tall and elegantly clothed in masses of double pink flowers. Occasionally a flock of parrots would fly past, wheeling above us in the azure sky, before regrouping and heading for the jungle just a mile away. I had an overpowering sense of peace and well-being as I lay, drifting lazily, cocooned amongst the blossoms. Beyond the circular driveway which skirted the lawn the house was utterly silent, although a dozen people had gone about their business there with noisy good humour barely half-an-hour before.

By degrees, a strange sound began to penetrate my lethargic state. It was a deep rhythmic rumble that seemed to come from the south.

'George,' I called out gently. 'Hey Georgie, can you hear that?'

He slept deeply with an angelic smile on his face, so I kicked him.

'Why did you wake me up?' he yelled. 'I was having a nice dream.'

'There's this strange sound coming from over there,' I replied, pointing to the south-east with an unsteady finger. 'Could it be a Jap flying thing?'

'The Japs are miles away. Anyway, our air force will shoot the lot down.' He closed his eyes and smiled again.

'That noise is getting louder,' I insisted. 'I'm scared.'

'You're a big girl, a sissy. I suppose you're going to cry now.' He gave me a condescending look. 'Go on, push off. I'm staying here.'

'George, come down quickly.'

The rumble had grown very loud and I was having difficulty breathing. Casually glancing towards the house I was astonished to see relatives, servants, even dogs, pouring out of the various doorways and sprinting towards the zig-zag trench under the loquat trees. Above the din the most encouraging sound I heard in those last ten minutes was the call of many voices: 'Stevie. Georgie. Where are you? Hurry, hurry. Stevie, Georgie. Air raid.'

Still puzzled, we gazed upwards. Then I saw them: dozens of silver birds in arrow formation silhouetted against a cloudless sky. I tried to attract George's attention but a loud wailing, which I learned too late was a warning siren, interrupted me.

My brother responded to the siren with a dazzling display of energy which left me staggered. He wriggled past me with amazing speed, all hands and legs and gasping breath, dropping straight down for the last six feet and bounding over the shrubs and roses as he headed for the shelter of the covered trench. Seeing him sprint like that was a joy, because a childhood accident had left George lame. But now he vanished from sight before I could even shout 'Wait for me.'

Suddenly a voice rang out across the garden.

'Stevie, run! Stevie, run! Jap bombers.'

Bombers? Japs? In a sudden flash I understood that these were the iron flying-birds — the first I had ever seen — that had killed Dickie and destroyed Rangoon and Mandalay. The planes were roaring almost overhead, but my air-gun was on the ground, out of my reach.

Managing to drop safely into a row of sweet peas I was down and sprinting, flashing over the flower-beds, waving my arms in fright and squealing like a stuck pig. Never in my life had I felt so exposed. It seemed my head would burst with the din of aeroplane engines and the loud chorus from the loquat trees: 'Run … run … run … Stevie.'

When I reached the trench I dived in head first, grabbed my mother and continued screaming loudly, ably supported by Maisie, as the bombs went off. The ground heaved as several huge explosions rippled away in a broad swathe towards the town and the station. In the semi-darkness of the trench, the heat, prayers and screams seemed to bind us all together in a communal frenzy. How I longed for the presence of a few fighting men from my family.

The Japanese missed me but I still remember the chilling sound of their bombs coming down before they exploded. We heard later that the bombers' real targets were Chiang Kai-shek, General Stilwell, General Alexander and Sir Reginald Dorman-Smith, who were supposed to be in Maymyo at this time. They failed to exterminate this quartet by a comfortable margin but nearly ended my story right here.

We climbed cautiously from the trench when the 'all clear' sounded. There were deep craters in the rich red earth of the field by the main road; the trail of destruction was marked by the row of toppled buildings and fires leading to the station. People were emerging from their ruined homes, and I can still hear their cries of despair. I picked up a piece of shrapnel from the assortment scattered at our feet, feeling the weight and running my finger over the jagged killing edge, my sense of bewilderment and fear about the future growing.

And so this eventful day ran its course – very different from the one I had expected. Watched over by my mother, George and I said our bedtime prayers, which were a great deal more sincere than the high-speed mumble we usually offered. Richard's death, the bombing of Maymyo, bad news from Mandalay and the knowledge that the enemy was closing in robbed me of any certainties.

*

Another week passed. It was midsummer and the earth so dry that the gardener spent half the day hauling water like Gunga Din from the public tap with the lion's head that stood in a clearing on the edge of our property. The way water poured out of the lion's mouth when he twisted the brass handle by the animal's ear never failed to amaze me.

On some nights the air was so still and hot that I felt I was suffocating. The image of cool running water became so overpowering that I could hear the ripple in my head and feel the splashes on my face. I used to call it brain fever.

During one such restless night I heard the sound of a heavy truck moving up our driveway. The headlamps shone through the open windows, cutting the darkness with bright shafts of light that moved across the wall like beams from a revolving lighthouse. Diving under the sheets, I listened as the sound of tyres crunching gravel finally came to a stop and the engine was switched off. There was a moment's silence, followed by the muffled sound of a familiar voice.

George and I tumbled out of bed and raced into the lounge, pushing the rest of the family aside as we leapt into Father's arms with shrieks of delight. It was good to feel his strength seeping into me again, his presence banishing the fears of the night. His uniform was powdered with dust and gave off a distinctive smell of sweat and petrol. We were still chattering delightedly when the door of the main bedroom opened, Mum appeared, and immediately burst into tears.

'William,' she sobbed. 'Richard … Richard … dead … killed.'

What a ghastly homecoming. I realised with a shock that whatever the reason for my father's sudden arrival, he did not know that his son had been killed. The joy in his eyes faded as he comforted my mother.

Someone tactfully led George and me away. We were told to be quiet and sent to bed again. There was little chance of falling asleep, my restlessness made worse by the drone of adult voices accompanied all night long by thuds and bumps as though furniture or boxes were being moved about.

What I saw next morning filled me with dismay. Clothes, documents and personal possessions lay scattered on the polished teak floors as though the house had been ransacked by robbers. Family and servants were rummaging through the items, ignoring my plaintive questions. In my parents' bedroom I stumbled across a mound of my mother's jewellery piled up in a shawl on the floor like a sacred offering. Gold necklaces, rings, buttons, bracelets, diamonds and other precious stones were mixed with gold sovereigns, pearls and fiery Mogok rubies. I was usually allowed to play with these while she dressed but this morning there was no frivolity. I walked past without a second glance.

In the dining-room I found my parents in emotional conversation with Queenie, Della and their children, but before I could take in what was being said, Maisie whisked me away.

'What's happening, Boozie?' I asked earnestly – Boozie was my nickname for Maisie. 'Is Mum all right now?'

But all she said was, 'Shush now. Get dressed, have something to eat and don't get in the way.'

'What's happening? Tell me! Tell me!'

'I'm not sure, but we may be going on a long trip,' she

replied. 'Take a few things in your bag.' Then she rushed off to find George.

Although I was only a child I knew there was a very serious crisis. Nevertheless, I wish now that someone had taken me into their confidence and given me a simple explanation, for had they done so I could have left my home with a more peaceful heart. But my feelings, it seemed, were irrelevant.

However, this was no moment for sulking and I hurriedly dressed myself in my best Sunday clothes. Then I took my secret wooden chest from under my bed. It was crammed with treasures: bright stones, pieces of glass, keys, used cartridges, matches, foreign stamps, assorted coins, penknives, metal odds-and-ends, a jamjar full of uncut Mogok rubies and my Sexton Blake annuals. As there was no time to sort through them I grabbed two handfuls and stuffed them into my blazer pockets, using a couple of large safety-pins to secure the openings. Then I left my bedroom for the last time.

In the lounge a gathering of family and servants, many of them weeping, made it obvious that some sort of departure was imminent. Queenie added to my confusion by kissing me good-bye, telling me that she was going to wait for her husband Rupert, while Della, who was married to my brother Willie, said she would wait for him. It made no sense, but no one paid the slightest attention to my pleas as the crowd moved relentlessly towards the front door.

I remember how desperate I felt when I saw the green-painted army truck with an armed driver at the wheel. I tugged Maisie's hand and bawled, 'Maisie, where are we going to?'

There was no reply.

Meanwhile my mother, white-faced and convulsed with weeping, was coaxed into the back of the truck, followed by George. I heard Maisie shout 'Stevie' but I broke away. Recklessly running to the front of the truck I pulled open the cab door and grasped my father's leg.

Almost incoherent with fright I gasped, 'Father! What's happening? Where are we going to?'

He looked down at me, but the softness of the night before had vanished; in its place was a scowl and hard unsmiling eyes. Here was a veteran soldier who had seen it all before in different lands and on different battlefields – the blood, violence and sacrifice, the waste and the loss. Forced to make a bitter decision involving his family and the home he had built, he was going to see it through, regardless of the opposition or the cost. I should have admired him, but I was too young to understand.

'We are going to China,' he replied harshly. 'Now get in the back of the truck.'

China? Did he say China? Why did they not tell me earlier? Where was China anyway? I felt tears burning my eyes.

I wanted to say, 'Help me, I'm scared. Please hold me.' But I had been brought up to understand that men did not cry, so I bit my lip and nothing came out but a suppressed moan.

'Hurry up Stephen,' he snapped. 'We've got to leave now.'

'Father – did you say China? What about Lindfield and Queenie and Della?'

With a bellow of annoyance he got out, picked me up roughly and thrust me into the back of the truck with the others. I remember feeling completely dazed and lost as the tail-board was slammed into place and pinned.

The engine burst into life, but before the truck could move Lal Bahadur, the gardener, grasped the tail-board and climbed in with us. The commotion was awful as people tried to drag him out, but he clung to the canvas roof and refused to leave, even when my father ordered him to.

'I have eaten your salt,' he shouted back in colloquial Hindustani. 'I will never leave you. Only death will separate us.'

As the row continued I curled up in a ball on the metal floor, wishing I was dead. But in the end my father relented, Lal Bahadur stayed, and the truck began to move down the driveway.

Now that my father could no longer see my face I wept openly. I remember straining my eyes to catch every detail, every colour, sound, shape and smell in these last few seconds. The cherry tree where George and I were dozing when the bombing started only a week before was still in full bloom. To the right was the eucalyptus tree on which we carved our names and in the middle distance I could see my faithful dog Socksie, bounding after the truck and barking at me with that characteristic toss of his head I knew so well. I tried to say something to him but my jaws had locked tight. It should never have happened like this: no word of farewell, no embrace to honour our years of friendship. Socksie's loyalty deserved more than this. But the truck picked up speed as it headed for the main road out of Maymyo and very soon Socksie was just a brown smudge in the distance. For a moment I saw the oak trees and the roof of Lindfield; then they were gone.

It had never crossed my mind for a second that the security of our home could be destroyed. Yet everything had vanished in a single bewildering morning and we were now vulnerable and rootless. Our world had shrunk to the confines of a three-ton army truck, a few suitcases, tin trunks, two boxes of hand-grenades and a mound of strange packing-cases under a tarpaulin. We had left behind a luxurious establishment, complete with cars, furnishings and personal belongings accumulated over decades. I was old enough at 11 to realise that we had crossed a crucial boundary. Staying alive had become a very dangerous game.

I looked at Maisie, studying her taut face and red-rimmed eyes.

'Father says we're going to China,' I said. 'Why didn't you tell me?'

'Sorry,' she said, and looked away.

'I'm scared,' I whispered, but she did not reply.

There was nothing more to say, nothing that would make any sense. I felt a strange sensation, as though I had been disembowelled, totally empty physically, spiritually and emotionally. I also made the startling discovery, as the truck headed eastwards to join the Burma Road to China, that I had lost the ability to pray. As for the Japanese, I vowed that no matter how long it took, I would get even. I would never forget. Never.

# 3  Chasing the Serpent

Shortly after dawn our truck turned east, following the main road that ran along the crest of a winding ridge. Below us the plains of Burma were laid out like a huge map, the light green squares of rice fields fringed by the darker green of forests and plantations. For the first time in my life I realised that the world was a much bigger place than I had ever imagined. Indeed, it seemed to go on for ever and ever. This was a momentous revelation for a small boy, equivalent to the discovery by early sailors that the world was round. But the adults were unmoved. They stared morosely into space, for they had seen it all before.

The road looked strangely familiar. I was certain I had seen it from a distance on a walk with my four sisters in the cool of an evening the previous year. We had reached a slight rise overlooking a valley when I saw a line of dappled lights weaving through the jungle about a mile away, like an incandescent serpent slithering in the dark.

Without any hesitation I stepped behind Janet in case it

turned out to be dangerous, emerging only when she told me rather scornfully that it was only the Burma Road and those lights were from lorries carrying military supplies all the way from Rangoon to Chungking. Sure enough, a faint rumbling sound drifted across the valley as the vehicles moved northwards in an unending stream. There were so many that when we walked past this viewing point several minutes later on our way back home, the weaving serpent was still alight and moving.

The notion that one day we would abandon our home and join those specks of light in desperate flight would have been greeted with complete disbelief that fine evening. Yet here we were on a cheerless morning, choking in the yellow dust churned up by hundreds of tyres as we bounced and rocked in our truck on the unmade stretches of road. The whole country was on the move and civilian cars, buses, lorries and carts, each one bulging with people and possessions, mingled with military vehicles, trucks and jeeps. My feeling of being in an asylum was reinforced by the awful rending sound of vehicle engines in torment and the searing heat under the thick canvas roof.

But despite the heavy traffic, we made steady progress throughout the morning because we were all pointed roughly in the same direction: away from the fighting. Clearly there would be no heroes manning the ramparts and fighting to the death on this stretch of the road, for the only vehicles moving south towards the Japanese forces at this stage of the conflict were either lost or suicidal.

After we had been on the road for a few hours, the jungle began to give way to more open countryside. I remember looking down on the undulating hills studded with small fields cut into the sloping sides and wondering if they grew poppies there, the opium sort that our cook's Chinese husband used to smoke. This man had died suddenly in hospital before my father could reach him, but came back that night to haunt us in a truly memorable performance when doors banged on their own, kitchen implements were flung about and gravel showered on the roof. Because of this peculiar disturbance I decided to sleep with my parents that night, but in the pitch darkness I woke to see a translucent figure bending over the bedside table next to my father. It took about an hour to get the family back to bed again after I raised the roof with my piercing screams. No one had any doubt that the cook's husband, though deceased, was still trying to say something to my father. I'm glad he gave up trying, because one visit was enough to turn me into a permanent insomniac.

Curiously, opium was also an ingredient, together with liquorice and unknown additives, of a wonderful cough mixture my father used to concoct in his surgery. It had a delightful bouquet to which George and I were very partial, and we used to quaff the elixir straight from the bottle whenever the grown-ups were foolish enough to leave it around. Consequently we were free from coughs and often quite docile.

About half-way to Lashio, the last large town before the Chinese border, we stopped at the crossroads near Hsipaw for a rest. The view of tranquil blue hills receding into the Shan States on the horizon was appealing: but it was a false picture. For unknown to us a Japanese armoured column had pushed through the disintegrating Chinese Sixth Army in the south and was, at this very moment, driving north-wards through those hills to seize this road junction and the town of Lashio. If they could get here within the next few days and cut the Burma Road to China, the Chinese Fifth Army in the central war zone would be trapped. Also in the bag would be the Brookes family.

Rather surprisingly, we were free from interference by Japanese aircraft all morning, but it was too good to last. Late that afternoon they suddenly appeared, skimming over the tree-tops and raking the road with machine-gun fire. The bombing raid on Maymyo a week before had so affected my nerves that from then on the sudden roar of an enemy aircraft overhead transformed me instantly into a burrowing animal. Now, true to form, I leaped over the tail-board and buried myself in thick undergrowth before the truck had even come to a standstill.

The whole convoy scattered, disgorging a mass of terrified people who vanished into the jungle. Tucked under my own private bush, I made myself as small as pos-sible as the Zeros went on the rampage, the clatter of their guns raking my raw nerves until I twitched and shivered. Finally the whizz-bangs stopped, but I stayed under my bush until my anxious father dragged me out. Several people had been killed and vehicles destroyed but our family group had suffered no casualties, though I seemed to have suddenly developed vertigo.

In the general confusion caused by weaving vehicles trying to rejoin the convoy after the attack, Father's arm got trapped between our truck and the one alongside. At first sight it looked as though his arm had been wrenched off and we feared the worst. But when the other drivers finally managed to prise him loose, we were relieved to find that he had suffered only severe lacerations and bruising. In a few minutes he had patched himself up with bandages and antiseptics, and was growling at Mum about 'useless drivers' and 'too much fussing'.

We were still on the road in the cool of the evening, monotonously picking up speed on the occasional straight sections, then inching carefully round the sharp hairpin-bends and crumbling verges to the next straight section for a repeat performance. Those who drove less carefully usually ended up at the bottom of a precipice or wrecked by the roadside. Presently the light began to fade and for a few moments the sky in the west was washed with red and gold and deepening shadows, before the scene vanished and the tropical night descended. I felt a sudden tremor of sadness as the headlamps of the vehicles were switched on, transforming the convoy into the incandescent serpent that my sisters and I had seen so long ago.

At about eight o'clock that night, having survived a gruelling drive of over one hundred miles in convoy and an air attack, we arrived at Lashio. My father decided to stop here although everyone else was trying to run away. The town was gripped by a communal frenzy which intensified with every hour. People were using anything from rusty cars to bullock carts, bicycles and human feet to get out of the way of the advancing Japanese column and the bombers. Debris from abandoned homes was everywhere; broken furniture, clothes and papers mingled with crashed vehicles. Black smoke filled the air, and the sound of human voices calling, talking, crying. This anarchic atmosphere was heightened by an undisciplined mob of Chinése soldiers who became violent when they were denied accommodation, food or transport.

Perhaps the scene was not so different from that described by Marco Polo more than 650 years earlier, when the Mongol horsemen of Kublai Khan fought a huge Burmese army on the border with China. The Burmese were defeated when their war elephants ran wild during the battle, the Mongols rode into Burma, overran Pagan and seized the Kingdom of Mien. Lashio was probably a tiny hamlet when they passed through it with fire and sword, down a jungle pathway that would one day be known as the Burma Road.

Over the next few days, during which we stayed with Colonel Lindsay of the Burma Public Health Service, the adults were caught up in this mêlée. I had no idea what they were up to, particularly my father, who used to drive off in the truck and return late in the evening. There was an airfield at the edge of the town but Mum refused to consider flying out to China or India without Father, and he refused to leave. After two days the option became academic when Japanese bombers destroyed the runway: the opportunity to get out by the easy route had been frittered away by my obstinate parents.

Meanwhile George and I, with nothing constructive to do, wandered nervously about this strange town. The question I kept asking myself was: why were we staying here day after day when our first priority, as I understood it, was to race the Japanese to China?

The first clue came to me some years later in an account by Dr Gordon Seagrave, the famous American medical missionary, of his time at the Baptist Mission hospital in a small town called Namkham near the Chinese border. He described meeting the Civil Surgeon of the area during a plague epidemic in 1940 – who was none other than our present host in Lashio, Colonel Lindsay. My father also knew Dr Seagrave through our family involvement in the American Baptist Church at Maymyo where Father preached, and the three men were all trained doctors and surgeons. Yet these links still did not entirely explain why we had made this risky journey to Lashio.

Then I remembered the strange packing cases under the tarpaulin in our vehicle and all it began to make sense. Clearly my father had brought vitally needed medical stores from the Medical Supply Depot at Fort Dufferin, since Mandalay was about to be overrun by the Japanese. Hence the three-ton truck.

Father arrived at a crucial moment when supplies were desperately short and casualties were mounting, especially amongst the Chinese troops. No doubt his talent as a surgeon was used in Lashio to treat the wounded: hence his absences during the day, while I fretted and agonised over the long delay in our flight to safety. Of course I knew that my father was a brave man – but I was like a calf in a butcher's shop, and the fearful sound of the Japanese mincing-machine, which grew closer and louder by the day, was terrifying. However, if an adult had explained all this to me fifty-seven years ago, I might have managed to enjoy this interlude, or at least to tolerate it.

An account by the Rev. Stanley Short, a missionary who had joined the Mobile Surgical Unit run by Dr Seagrave, describes how they passed through Lashio at this period, spending a night in the house of the Burmese Baptist Pastor, U Williams – the very house at which, by this time, we were staying. Rev. Short mentions the stirring service of prayer and hymn-singing held in the guest-room that night. By the light of a flickering oil lamp, Burmese, Karen and English voices were raised in song while pandemonium reigned outside. All I can recall of the occasion are a few words from a Karen hymn.

A few days later came the news everyone had been dreading: the Japanese had broken through the Chinese forces and were now astride the Burma Road. They had won the race, thrusting northwards for over 300 miles to block the road which we had used a few days earlier. We were now effectively cut off from our home, and our life at Lindfield passed into history.

On the Burma side of the road-block, the troops of the Chinese Fifth Army who had failed to get back in time were now trapped. We were later to witness their destruction, hundreds of their bodies littering the swamps and jungle trails as they died of disease and starvation in the hell of the Hukawng Valley. But for the people of Lashio the fight was over and the town lay open to the enemy, straight down the Burma Road.

Very soon the Japanese would be on the outskirts of the town. I could not sleep at night for hideous thoughts of the violence to come. It was too late now to run and our eleven-day advantage had been dissipated by my father. The airfield was unusable, the streets were silent as families cowered in the dark behind bolted doors and windows. Nothing moved in the dead town. The moment of reckoning had come and I shivered in the dark, wondering what a bayonet in the stomach would really feel like.

I do not know what prompted my father to move. Perhaps he felt he had done his duty and there was nothing more to be gained by staying. It may have been divine providence or a final realisation of the danger his family was in. Maybe it was my mother's pleading, or the old fighting spirit stirring again, but whatever it was it came just in time.

Suddenly my parents were rushing through the rooms with torches. There were urgent voices: we were going to make a run for it in the dark. I couldn't believe my father could be so crazy and I remember saying 'Bloody hell!' several times under my breath. But I moved fast, gathering up my things in seconds, instantly elated by the prospect of flight. Our possessions were thrown into the truck, we piled into the back, doors slammed shut and the engine sprang to life. It was half-past-four in the morning, pitch black and cold, as we raced through the town looking for the road that led to China.

From somewhere in the darkness came the faint sound of rifle fire – could be Chinese, could be Japanese. There were no clear thoughts in my head, just a swirling mass and a constriction in my chest. In the stillness of the night the engine of the racing truck roared like a tank on the loose. Houses and shacks flashed past, caught for an instant in the headlights before vanishing into the darkness behind us. I was certain that death was round the next corner. Was that a Jap or just a pile of discarded clothes? And that bang – was it the truck or a shot? And why, oh why, was it taking so long?

In reality it took only a few minutes of reckless driving

and then, suddenly, we were through, lurching round bends and dodging roadside trees as we sped into the countryside. We'd made it, but only by a whisker. Probably we only survived because the Chinese were not alert at that hour of the morning, or maybe the Japanese were not bothering since they had achieved their objective of blocking the road behind the Chinese. Gradually a sense of sanity returned and I risked a smile in the dark, but this was definitely an experience I did not want to repeat.

We were free! We were alive! Curled up on the metal floor of the truck with my head in my mother's lap I slept the sleep of the reprieved prisoner, astonished yet again by the peace and strength that flowed from holding another human being.

I woke at dawn to the sound of singing and clapping as my mother led the others in a round of stirring Baptist hymns: 'When the roll is called up yonder' (clap, bang, clap); 'Happy day, oh happy day' (clap, clap, clap); 'Hold the fort for I am coming' (bang). So it went on all morning and when our voices gave out we spent hours gossiping as though we had just discovered one another.

In this relaxed mood my mother entertained us with rousing tales of Burmese kings, queens and ministers caught up in palace intrigues and wars. She told us stories about the spirits and weretigers in the jungle, and incredible anecdotes of the early years when my father was posted to remote towns as Assistant Civil Surgeon.

At this point I realised with a sickening shock that our gardener Lal Bahadur, who had come with us from

Maymyo, was missing. I pleaded with Mum to let us stop the truck and go back to Lashio, but she was evasive.

'He's with his own people where it's much safer,' she said with a soothing smile.

Yet I felt upset and ashamed by this turn of events. Lal Bahadur had been my companion from my earliest childhood and his loss was another broken link with Lindfield. Clearly nothing could be taken for granted in this war.

Soon we drew up on the outskirts of a little town called Kutkai, where all traffic had come to a halt. The road ahead was blocked by hundreds of Chinese troops trying to disentangle two formations of transport, guns and armour. Part of this force had begun to deploy across the road and into the surrounding countryside to halt the Japanese advance, while the remainder, in an attempt to get back across the Chinese border to Yunnan as quickly as possible, had started to move through them in the opposite direction, causing immense confusion. We fretted and fumed but it was no good. For the moment the stationary convoy, strung out for miles on the open hillsides round the town, was a gift-wrapped target for a Japanese bomber or fighting patrol. I knew it would not be long before the sound of gunfire and explosions would rock the valley.

Luckily we were only buzzed twice. The first time there was so much noise from the troops and vehicles that a pair of fighter planes were overhead before anyone noticed them. There was a frantic scramble away from the vehicles to find cover under trees, bushes and depressions in the hillside. But the plane made only a single pass, shooting up something just ahead of us before turning northwards towards the American airfield at Loiwing. About five miles further on there was a repeat performance when a brace of fighters appeared from nowhere and sprayed the tail-end of the convoy before disappearing. These aircraft were probably on specific missions. Otherwise they would have stayed and knocked the hell out of the convoy.

While we waited for the 'all-clear', a couple of villains in shabby Chinese uniforms started to climb into the back of our truck. Perhaps they thought that taking on two defence-less women and two boys was better than fighting the Japanese army. But they made a mistake. Before I could yell a warning to my father in the driver's cab, my mother was transformed into a raging virago. She sprang to the attack, shaking her slippers in their faces, screeching and swearing in filthy Burmese like a street trader. Her reaction was so violent and unexpected that the soldiers fled instantly, while we three children cowered away from her in the recesses of the truck. We stayed there for several minutes until she stopped snarling and swishing her slippers about.

Of course we all knew that to be beaten with slippers is an insult and a disgrace in Asia. But for a man to be beaten by a woman wielding slippers is a disgrace approaching mortal sin. It was a risk the two louts dared not take in full view of their cronies – the cowards. When it was safe for us to emerge, I looked at my mother with considerable pride and a touch of caution. With a temper like that she might even stop the Japanese singlehandedly. For the rest of the day I felt she was the bravest woman in the world.

Finally, in the early afternoon, the road was opened and the convoy drove through the town towards the Chinese border. Thirty miles further on we came to the turning for Namkham where Dr Seagrave's hospital was located. The road looked deserted, though there was no telling what lay concealed in the jungle. My father, anxious to find out whether the hospital was still functioning, changed his mind only when we protested loudly that we were worn out. It was just as well, for though we didn't know it, Seagrave had left. We found out later that he had joined General Stilwell's forces on the Irrawaddy river a few days earlier, when it was clear that the Japanese advance could not be held. They had retreated westwards through the Chin hills, following the tracks that eventually led to India.

The excitement of the last few days, coupled with the swaying of the truck, began to make me feel nauseous again. I had hardly drifted into a disturbed sleep, with my head bouncing on a suitcase, before I was startled by George shaking my arm. There was a broad smile on his face. He told me we had reached China.

Bleary-eyed and lethargic, I ignored the general euphoria, but I remember our truck passing under a nondescript wooden archway decked with flowers, green leaves and flags. If this was the gateway to peace and happiness for which we had sacrificed our home, I was unimpressed. There was a board with strange writing on it which Maisie said was Chinese, though she did not sound very convincing. We joined the long queue of frustrated drivers halted at the military and customs checkpoints. The interminable delays and arguments over documentation were intensely boring. When it was our turn, my father discreetly slipped the guard a fistful of notes and we were waved through with a smile and a salute. This was the first time I had witnessed the magical Asian process by which rupee notes are instantly transformed into documentation.

After a short distance we came to an open square lined with jacaranda trees where we stopped to stretch our cramped limbs. We were covered from head to foot in a coating of fine red dust – except for my father who, having spent the entire journey in the driver's cab, still looked remarkably cool and smart in his uniform and Sam Browne belt. I decided then and there what I wanted to be when I grew up – and it was not an engine-driver.

Our Chinese driver strolled towards us smoking a cigarette.

'This wanting,' he said, without removing the stub from his mouth.

'Wanting? Wanting what?' asked my father patiently.

'This wanting.' He jabbed a finger at the decrepit buildings on one side of the square.

'Perhaps he wants a room,' suggested my mother helpfully.

George whispered 'Rubbish' in my ear, but I kept my mouth shut. I was too tired to be clever.

The poor man was obviously trying to communicate something important but our exhausted brains had finally stopped working. For several seconds he glared at us as if we were a class of backward children. Then he let out a sigh of utter frustration and pointed to a road sign which we had missed. In English capital letters it spelt quite simply the word 'WANTING'. It was the name of the town. We giggled foolishly as he stalked away towards a tea stall, muttering a string of ominous-sounding Chinese words after which he spat.

I was not impressed by Wanting or its tea and cakes. When I sampled the favourite local drink, which was plain hot water, it reminded me so vividly of the time when I was sick that I retched automatically. If this was China they could keep it. There were no round felt tents, yaks or exotic caravans. None of the wild horsemen dressed in silks, with droopy moustaches and long pigtails that my *Boy's Own* magazine had described so tantalisingly.

Instead of exotic Mongols there were more dusty armoured vehicles, artillery and lorries, with the usual crowd of disorderly soldiers in yellow uniforms and puttees. I had a nasty feeling that my father's brittle temper combined with my mother's tendency to slipper-waving could ignite a civil war before the day was through.

# 4  Sawbwa Fang of Mangshih

Soon after tea we left Wanting and began the winding climb up to the small town of Chefang, which we reached in less than an hour. The air was fresher up here and it was pleasantly cool in the fading amber glow of the late afternoon sun. Beyond Chefang the road passed through a range of treeless conical hills of a kind I had never seen before, except in Chinese paintings on calendars and postcards. The crests of some had been weathered away, leaving exposed cliffs of reddish rock split by deep crevices in which scattered groves of hardy pine trees clung perilously. They scented the air in the valley with the distinctive smell of resin, redolent of Christmases past and toasted marshmallows by the charcoal fire at home.

On the brow of one of the hills were rows of white stone slabs which Mum said were the graves of the local people's ancestors. She also told me that when we reached Mangshih we were going to stay with an old family friend called Fang Yu-chi who was the Sawbwa of Mangshih. As usual I was told to behave myself and keep out of sight, so I prepared myself for some more nasty examples of adult folly. Left to themselves they always came up with a crazy plan that was bound to get us killed.

The Sawbwas were hereditary rulers of small states inhabited by the Shans, a branch of the Mongolian people. Cheerful and prosperous, the Shans were known by such picturesque names as Lords of the Sunset, Lords of the Sunrise, or Lords of the Hills. Over a thousand years before they had ruled a kingdom in Yunnan called Nanchao, but were driven southwards by the Tartars in the thirteenth century and spread into Burma, Siam and Indo-China. For a while they ruled Burma but were soon pushed back into an area of several thousand square miles on Burma's eastern frontier known as the Shan States. Mangshih, our destination, was a state of about 2,000 square miles on the Chinese side of the border.

I remembered the Sawbwa of Mangshih clearly, because he always stayed with us at Lindfield when he visited Burma. He was of medium height, quite slender, with a sallow face, short grey hair and a couple of flashing gold-capped teeth which I found fascinating. He was always smartly dressed in a Western suit, but what placed him in my highest category of celebrity – higher even than my cowboy heroes Tom Mix and Gene Autrey – was the length of the nail on the little finger of his left hand. It must have been two inches long and was curved, like a claw. I have no idea why he grew it to such a length, though George and I invented some scurrilous reasons.

The Sawbwa had recently taken a 19-year-old Eurasian called Ida as his second wife. She was a sparkling, high-spirited girl, exhaustingly talkative and the antithesis of the Sawbwa's first wife, a Chinese lady a little older than himself. When the Sawbwa stayed with us, Ida and my sisters would crowd into Marie's bedroom where they whispered and giggled incessantly about matters which eluded me, though I pressed my ear hard against the door.

Occasionally the Sawbwa was accompanied by his secretary Chin Lee, who I remember particularly because of a comical episode which enhanced my reputation as a reliable watch-dog at the age of 10. One night after dinner at Lindfield he and one of my sisters decided to take a stroll in the garden – something which, in those far-off days, was governed by strict rules of decorum. I was sent with them as a chaperon, better known by my sisters as a 'bloody lemon'. As the three of us strolled through the dark in stately fashion I tried to ignore the squeals and fumbles of my two companions behind me. After several perspiring minutes, the frustrated Chin Lee decided to try to get rid of me by offering me an incentive. Taking out his thick wallet he gave it to me with a knowing smile and a quick tilt of the head. The unspoken message was 'Get lost, kid!'.

I can still clearly remember the huge wad of crinkly rupee notes with big numbers on them. But to a small boy they were just bits of paper. I only understood small denomination copper coins and there were none of those. So I handed the wallet back, saying politely, 'No thank you'.

The couple's unexpected reaction alarmed me. My sister fumed and shuddered like a volcano while the stunned Chin Lee tried to cuff me on the head as we marched back to the house. The atmosphere was poisonous.

'That child is a pest and I never want to see him again,' said my furious charge, pointing a quivering finger at me. I could not understand what all the fuss was about, as I would gladly have disappeared and left her alone with her admirer for one anna. Grown-ups were really quite childish at times, I decided.

Chin Lee became famous after the war as the author of *The Flower Drum Song*, which was put on in London's West End some time during the late 1950s or early '60s. I remember standing outside the theatre debating whether to see it, but at the time I had no idea the author was the same Chin Lee who had failed to tempt me with a fortune in rupees when I was a boy.

About the same time I discovered a book written by Chin Lee called *A Corner Of Heaven*, in which he vividly described Mangshih and the life of the Sawbwa and Ida. But even more fascinating was his description of my parents and of our visit to Mangshih during the retreat from Burma in 1942.

After an exhausting thirteen-hour journey we reached Mangshih on 26 April. Night had fallen when we drove up to a warm welcome at the Sawbwa's palace, known as a *yamen*, or a *haw* in Shan. It was a large rambling building in the classical Chinese style, with gracefully curved tiled roofs and red-pillared halls. The rooms were dark and high-ceilinged, the air still and heavy with the lingering smell of camphor and incense sticks. The floors were scattered with sumptuous handmade carpets while ornate antique chairs and tables, lacquered ornaments and several large brass spittoons filled the empty spaces. Beneath the sombre paintings which covered the walls the staff shuffled noiselessly on slippered feet, adding to the atmosphere of genteel gloom. Occasionally an old lady, with her feet bound into tiny spindles like the hooves of a delicate fawn, would hobble past with a tray of jasmine tea in tiny porcelain cups. I found it all distinctly spooky and took care never to let George out of my sight for the duration of our stay.

The following evening the Sawbwa invited us to a lavish dinner with Ida, Chin Lee and some military personnel. George and I were seated at a separate table, presumably to shield the other diners from our antics with chopsticks. We avoided the fifty-year-old preserved eggs, which were black and repulsive, but the roast duck, steamed fish and sweet bean-cakes were delicious. However, the high point of the dinner for us was munching pine-seeds and spitting the residue into spitoons – a new and fascinating pastime which we pursued energetically. But our fun was cut short when we were sent off early to bed so that the adults could get down to the serious business of discussing the war. When we had to shake hands with the Sawbwa and thank him for his hospitality, we were relieved that his grisly claw was on his left hand and not his right.

Next day I tried to persuade my mother to tell me about their discussion, but she was evasive and unhelpful. Maisie was more forthcoming, but what she told me was so grotesque that I was immediately sorry I had asked. It seemed that the initial plan had been for us children and my mother to continue the journey to Kunming, from where a plane would fly us to India. Meanwhile, unhampered by us, my father would get on with his war and meet us in India in due course. Predictably, this plan was rejected out of hand by my mother. She would not leave him. 'Until death us do part' was a vow she had made on her wedding day and by God, she meant to honour it. She was so like me when she was being pig-headed that I found it quite endearing. However, because of her unshakeable stand, we were all going back to Burma tomorrow, driving in our truck towards the advancing Japanese army. Yes, that's right – towards the Japanese.

Even after fifty-seven years, I can find no justification for this fateful decision. George and Maisie were probably conditioned to accept their elders' edicts as a matter of course, because that was the way of family life before the war. But I was still a free spirit, and bombers, bayonets, explosions and bow-legged Japanese frightened the living daylights out of me. So I ranted and raved for the rest of the day and made myself thoroughly ill. But the decision was final: the family must not be split up. We would live together – and die together.

And so, in the pale morning light of 28 April, we turned our backs upon China and safety. Bidding farewell to Ida and the Sawbwa, we retraced our route down the perilous road up which we had so recently travelled. When I pointed out that we seemed to have fewer possessions in the truck I was told that we had left two trunks at Mangshih for safe-keeping, which we would collect when the war was over. I do not know what was in the trunks but as they were clearly important to our family I guess they included family papers, photographs, official documents and jewels. Perhaps they are still there, mouldering slowly into dust in the dark and lonely ruin that was once the *yamen* of the Sawbwa of Mangshih.


The return journey to Burma was understandably free from traffic since the convoys, quite sensibly, were going in the opposite direction. There was no hymn-singing, clapping or idle chatter as we drove through Chefang and down to the border at Wanting. A bleak feeling of inevitability had descended on George and me as we sat side-by-side. I was seething with suppressed anger and frustration for I could see no sense in this pointless journey. The heat, dust and military activity increased steadily as the afternoon dragged by and twice we scurried for shelter when Japanese bombers appeared overhead. The whizz-bangs beat on my fragile nerves, bringing back my vertigo, which had disappeared for the last few days, with a vengeance. Staying alive was becoming a problem again.

We passed the turning to Dr Seagrave's hospital at Namkham once more and headed back down the road towards Lashio, a hundred miles further on, in Japanese territory. About half-way there, somewhere past the town of Kutkai and near the village of Hsenwi, we rounded a bend in the road and drove straight into a Chinese army road-block.

This was designed to halt the Japanese advance up the Lashio road. No one was prepared for the sudden arrival of the Brookes family, travelling in the opposite direction. We came to a lurching halt within a few feet of a lorry lying on its side across the road. In the scrub on either side were troops bristling with arms, while beyond we could see the outlines of armoured vehicles.

Within seconds we were surrounded by a screaming mob of soldiers waving an assortment of weapons, some of which they fired over our heads. My father was in his officer's uniform but they hauled him out of the cab. I heard him trying to shout an explanation above the awful din but the soldiers were so worked up I was certain they were going to shoot us – and I would not have blamed them.

By and by the tumult died down. The troops were finally convinced that we were not part of a cunning Japanese plan to attack them from the rear. We were just stupid tourists wandering about in a battlefield for want of something better to do on a fine afternoon. Eventually they drifted back to their trenches. It had been a close call.

A few minutes later Father appeared at the back of the truck, ashen-faced and ill-tempered. His loaded pistol was still in his hand but on finding us unharmed he thrust it into his belt. Then followed a conversation which I shall remember as long as I live.

'Pass me a box of hand-grenades,' Father said.

Maisie and I fumbled about, confused and sweaty-handed but too scared to ask questions. Eventually we found something we assumed was a hand-grenade box and dragged it forward. He prised the lid open, took out two grenades and put them in his pockets.

Then he said, 'There are Japanese in the jungle near here. If we run into trouble, pull the pins out and throw these grenades. All right?'

We nodded automatically like a pair of puppets, but our eyes must have betrayed our terror and total ignorance of what we were supposed to do.

'Well done,' he said warmly.

Then he turned on his heel, got back into the cab, the truck reversed and we headed back to Kutkai.

Maisie and I looked at one another aghast. All I knew about grenades was that you did something and counted to three – or was it five? But why or under what circumstances I did not know. I suspected that if you got it wrong you blew yourself up.

'Oh, my God,' said Maisie, in her usual helpful way, twitching nervously. 'What shall we do Stevie?'

There was only one possible answer. 'Forget about it,' I whispered and closed the box carefully.

We reached Kutkai late that evening and stayed once again in the house of the Burmese pastor U Williams. My father went to look for Colonel Lindsay who was also in the town, but I was too physically and emotionally exhausted to register anything else about that night. I was still half asleep when we set off at dawn, back up the Burma Road again towards China.

When I felt able to sit up and take notice of our surroundings, we had reached the familiar turning to Namkham and Dr Seagrave's hospital. This time, instead of following the road to the Chinese border, we took the one that led to Namkham and the American airfield at Loiwing. At 4.30 that afternoon we drove into the hospital grounds, to find a scene of frenzied activity as the remaining missionaries and hospital staff dismantled the equipment and prepared to leave. They told us that although the airfield had been heavily bombed the day before, a group had managed to fly out to India. The rest were planning to follow in the last plane at dawn next day.

More alarming still was the news of the Japanese advance.

Lashio, we learned, had fallen and there were unconfirmed reports that the enemy had pushed on to the road-block. If the Chinese could not hold them there they could be at Namkham within a day. Even more disturbing was news of their encircling move through the hills beyond the Namtu silver mines which could bring them to Namkham and the American airfield within a few hours.

For the second time in twenty-four hours we would have to move fast to keep ahead of them. I hoped my father would not get any more bright ideas about rearguard actions with hand-grenades. I was not in the mood for heroics, especially as the tropical night had descended and both Maisie and I were scared of the dark. So it was with considerable relief that we heard him tell Mother that we would cross the Shweli river bridge immediately and drive through the night to the frontier town of Bhamo.

It was a fortunate decision for, as we later heard, the enemy surprised the guards on the bridge next day and killed them all. The bridge over the Shweli river was taken and the Japanese were right behind us again.

We emerged from the hills above Bhamo just as dawn was breaking. Wisps of smoke from the houses drifted lazily across the lattice of paddy-fields in the valley through which the Irrawaddy flowed. On this peaceful morning it was comforting to see the light of the rising sun dancing on the swirling water. The serene unfolding motion of the sweeping current evoked memories of Paul Robeson singing 'Ole Man River', his deep voice floating across the veranda at Lindfield in the soft twilight from our wind-up gramophone with the fluted horn. There could hardly have been a greater contrast between the placid permanence of the river and our own uncertain human condition.

We threaded our way through the outskirts of the town, avoiding the refugees by the waterfront, but it was Lashio all over again. The town was going through a communal nervous breakdown as the enemy assembled in the jungles for the final push. The Chinese troops, cut off by the Japanese armoured column at Lashio, clogged the town and the roads out of it as they scrambled to get home via the mountain tracks further north. You could smell the fear, and it was infectious. A whiff of it could release all my pent-up misgivings, and I never found an antidote – though clinging tightly to my mother or singing a few bars of a Baptist hymn usually gave some relief. Apart from Maisie and myself, everyone in the truck seemed to have become immune to it, gazing listlessly at the confusion as we drove slowly down a narrow street to Bhamo's Circuit House.

These buildings, also known as dak bungalows, were a wonderful British invention. Their existence made it possible for officials to travel to the remotest corners of their possessions in India and Burma, and always arrive at an oasis of comfort, where they would be pampered with baths, clean sheets, 'proper' food and a tumbler of whisky by the resident custodian. However the isolation of many of them made them ideal places for stirring adventures, and the *Wide World Magazine*, now regrettably out of print, used to carry regular stories of the unusual experiences of visitors. Chief amongst these were encounters with wild beasts ranging from poisonous snakes to man-eating tigers and berserk elephants. But paranormal phenomena and attacks from natives were far from uncommon.

During our visit, the only strange occurrence was the invasion of one bedroom late one night by a massive army of black ants. Quite suddenly we noticed them sweeping into the room through a hole in the floorboards. Within a couple of minutes the floor was awash under a pool of dark, glistening ants, moving rapidly like a single organism. The edges expanded silently outwards as thousands more ants surged in, enveloping the ceiling and walls in a sinister black shadow. It was a ghostly sight, particularly by the dim light of the kerosene lantern which was all the custodian had, because of the power cuts. There was also a curious smell in the room which probably came from the ants, though we did not stay long enough to identify it, fleeing unashamedly to the far end of the bungalow with our belongings. The Burmese custodian was surprisingly unperturbed. He coolly locked the door, assuring us that all would be well in the morning. He was right of course, for when we looked into the room next morning there was not an ant in sight.

It was 1 May and we had been on the run for over two weeks, though it seemed more like two years. I suppose by now I should have grown used to the adults' habit of abruptly announcing their decisions to me with an air of casual detachment. George tended to take this in his stride and co-operated willingly, but I always bristled with indignation at being taken for granted. So I scowled at my mother as she explained that this evening we would board a steamer of the Irrawaddy Flotilla Company, which would take us downstream to the town of Katha. From Katha we would take the train northwards to Myitkyina: assuming of course that such things as railway-lines, engines and drivers still existed after the non-stop Japanese air attacks.

There was nothing north of Myitkyina except two tiny border outposts. Beyond them were the snow-covered mountains of Tibet and China. You did not need to be a clever adult to realise that once we were in Myitkyina the game was up, for to the north, east and west of the town were impassable rivers, mountains and jungles. In other words, it was a rat trap.

Mother's news was not conducive to a jolly breakfast. Moreover, it did not make sense. I had overheard the custodian advising someone that there was a motorable track which ran northwards straight to Myitkyina. It was only half as long as the route proposed by my mother, but she would not listen. I still remember the quick flush of irritation that crossed her face, followed by a barely perceptible flicker of understanding.

'Don't talk rubbish,' she said gently, as she left the room. 'Just make sure you're ready.'

But in those few seconds, a subtle exchange of chemistry had taken place between us that fundamentally changed our relationship – I felt that for a moment my mother had accepted that I could be a responsible player in this adventure, someone she could rely on.

That evening we were driven down to the jetty on the Irrawaddy where our few possessions were unloaded. Father then ordered our Chinese driver to return to his unit. He had been a vital member of our group for over two weeks and I was sorry to see him go, especially since without him and our own transport we would be unable to outrun the Japanese. Indeed, they were right behind us, advancing along the same road we had so recently used, crushing all attempts by the Chinese rearguard to stop them.

The scene at the jetty was one of utter confusion as hundreds of people tried to board the last boats before the enemy arrived. Ours looked a peculiar shape to me until I realised that it was a ferry boat with two large flat-topped barges strapped one on either side. There was not a square inch on this contraption that was not occupied by a human body or a pile of baggage. Father had secured a cramped space that passed for a cabin, but as there was no room for the baggage we piled it up outside. It did not take us long to realise that the crowd was dispersing our belongings as they tried to find a little deck-space. Something would have to be done, and quickly.

My father now decided that each person was to be responsible for carrying his or her own belongings, since we no longer had a truck or a driver. Anything we could not personally carry was to be thrown into the river. It was left to each of us to choose between sentimental items and those essential for survival.

When the dock gates were closed the boat pulled away from the bank and anchored off-shore for the night, which seemed to calm those on board. Before long the hectic activity ceased, and was replaced by the hum and chatter of relaxed voices and the smell of smouldering cheroots. It was time to settle our problem.

I closed my eyes when my mother and father left the cabin with their baggage, shutting out harsh reality with memories of home: wrestling with Socksie in a pile of fallen oak leaves; roasting sweet potatoes in the embers of a fire in my den; the amazing sight of ice on a saucer of sugared water which Father left out on the lawn one December night; carol singers with lanterns at Christmas – golden days, all replaced now by fear and uncertainty.

At last my parents reappeared and it was our turn. George and I were each helped into two pairs of shorts and two shirts, then we carried our bags to the ship's rail and slung some of the contents overboard. I had an awful feeling of doom as my things went. I still had my school blazer with both pockets stuffed with treasure but I cannot remember if George kept anything.

Finally it was Maisie's turn. I helped her carry her baggage through the crowd and stood beside her at the ship's rail as she opened her case and began to throw her belongings overboard. I could feel the tension mounting and see the deepening despair on her tearful face as each item went. Even so I was unprepared for the shock when she finally drew out her magnificent white silk wedding-dress and pushed it through the railings. I watched in horror as the dress floated briefly on the surface like a luminous ghost. Then it began to sink, slowly and silently, in the dark waters of the Irrawaddy. The sound of Maisie's wrenching sobs made me utterly desolate. For a moment I saw the swirling current caress the dress, then it slipped gently downstream and was taken by the river.

My sister had been on the point of marrying Frank, a soldier in the King's Own Yorkshire Light Infantry, but the Japanese invasion had wrecked their plans, sweeping them in different directions: him to the front line and her on this desperate journey. Perhaps she had kept this token in the hope that by some miracle they would meet, but until the lights came on again, marriage was a fantasy.

Early next morning we sailed down the Irrawaddy, but for me the magic of the great river rolling down to the sea had disappeared and I felt ill-tempered and out of sorts. Too much had happened too soon and it was hard to adjust to the incessant bad news. Lack of proper rest did not help either. I did my best to forget as I gazed fixedly at the distant fields and coconut groves, but all I could see was Maisie's white silk wedding dress sinking, again, and again. It was that sort of day.

Within three days of our departure downstream, all resistance crumbled and Bhamo was taken by the Japanese. In a few days they would link up with their forces moving northwards through the centre of Burma to dominate the Irrawaddy for a thousand miles to the sea. They would then move quickly northwards to Myitkyina along the motorable track. It was small comfort to know the custodian had been right after all. Even so, could our roundabout route still get us to Myitkyina before the Japanese? The outlook was not promising, yet curiously, as our options dwindled so our will to survive and determination to fight began to grow.

Night was drawing in when we anchored at Katha. Covering a distance of eighty miles in twelve hours, we had sailed down a huge loop of the Irrawaddy in a south-westerly direction towards the main Japanese army. A sense of humour was obviously essential for a full appreciation of our escape so far. We had travelled over 700 miles in eighteen days, describing a majestic circle, all the way east and then all the way back west, so that we were now only 150 miles north of our home in Maymyo as the crow flies. The Japanese army was behind us now, heading north to our common destination of Myitkyina.

As soon as the boat docked a tangled mass of men, women and screaming children, carrying pots, pans, chickens, sacks of food and mounds of bedrolls disembarked. In less than an hour they were swallowed up by the night as they hurried away from the river to begin the next stage of their escape. We should have joined them, but my father decided that as we were not in a fit state to continue the journey we would spend the night on board. What a relief it was to have some space to lie down and stretch our limbs without being trampled by a refugee or crushed by baggage. I sandwiched myself tightly between George and Maisie and despite the noise of the river traffic, the hard teak deck and the fleas, I slipped instantly into a deep and untroubled sleep.

Early next morning we breakfasted on sweet rice cakes and green tea which my mother bought from a nearby stall. Refreshed, we boarded a native sampan to ferry us to the west bank of the river but as soon as we cast off I lost my enthusiasm for this form of transport. It was not just that the deck was about three inches above the waterline or that I was a non-swimmer: it was the shock of experiencing the awesome power of the Irrawaddy river at close quarters from what was, in effect, a flimsy wooden bathtub. The words of the hymn 'O God our help in ages past' flashed through my mind as the seething brown water swirled against the hull. Too frightened to watch, I closed my eyes tightly and sat perfectly still while the wheezing boatman fought the current. After about twenty minutes of sheer terror a dull thud on the hull indicated that we had arrived.

Safe on shore again we strapped our baggage on our shoulders and set off in single file to find the railway station. Japanese Zeros were active in the sky above Katha and it was clearly unwise to linger in the town. When we finally discovered the station we found a miracle waiting for us – an ambulance train, fully steamed up and about to depart for Myitkyina. It was overflowing with wounded soldiers, but when those in charge realised that my father was an army surgeon, we were received enthusiastically.

Of all our recent journeys, this 100-mile trip to Myitkyina in a packed ambulance train took first prize for discomfort. The lack of ventilation in the congested carriages seemed to concentrate the foul smell of human bodies and disinfectants. Everywhere you looked you saw something unpleasant oozing out of bandages and wounds. The atmosphere was so appalling that it was a relief to leap out whenever the train was halted by marauding Japanese planes. If it was a choice between being killed instantly by a machine-gun bullet or suffocating in this charnel house, we preferred the former every time. My father was kept busy throughout the journey, tending the wounded and disposing of the dead. But this was his profession so he had no horror of delving in warm entrails up to his elbows or chopping off limbs. We, on the other hand, were still at the stage of fainting at the sight of blood.

The agony grew steadily worse as the train made its ponderous way northwards through the night. We rose with the sun, fully expecting we were about to arrive, but soon dis-covered that we were only halfway there. We travelled the whole of the next interminable day, harassed by Japanese planes and never far from puking, and arrived that evening more dead than alive. We were still ahead of the Japanese – but only by a whisker.

# 5  *Fly Me to India*

So this was Myitkyina. In the late evening light the warren of wooden buildings with their corrugated iron roofs and dimly-lit interiors looked about as welcoming as the ghostly palace ruins of Mandalay. Had it really been worth such continuous battering of mind and body to reach this forlorn outpost between the mountainous borders of India, Tibet and China, I wondered. Well, we had at least won our 800-mile race with the Imperial Japanese Army. They were seldom more than seventy-two hours behind us, though their exciting spurt near the Chinese border had briefly reduced our lead to a spine-tingling two hours.

With our remaining possessions piled on our backs, we walked slowly through the dark streets to find the Circuit House. After the awful boat and train journeys of the last four days we felt utterly drained as we stumbled into the sanctuary of the building. Ignoring the offer of food, we made our way to our quarters and the luxury of a quiet family bedroom with soft beds, clean sheets and running water. After a perfunctory wash we slipped under the blankets and were asleep in seconds.

This was the deep, revitalising sleep that our mistreated bodies had longed for since leaving China. But we slept too well, for at dawn Colonel Tandon, one of my father's colleagues, arrived in his car to take us to the airfield – and we were not ready. Like the five foolish virgins of St Matthew's Gospel, we had no oil in our lamps – no alarm clock, no breakfast and no sense. Though we pleaded with him to wait a few minutes, Colonel Tandon left without us. His anxiety that any delay would jeopardise his chance of a plane to India was perfectly understandable since the Japanese forces were closing in rapidly on Myitkyina, the last operational airfield in Burma.

Nevertheless, the chilling sense of failure was hard to shake off. We had come so far, through so many trials and tribulations, yet when salvation arrived in the form of a lift to the airfield and a plane to India – we were asleep. We had finally blown it.

We sat silently round the breakfast table in the Circuit House, painfully aware that from now on things could only get worse. The hope of a happy ending to our story had vanished, and I was haunted by the fear that I would be unable to face a Japanese bayonet with courage. I desperately wanted my parents to know that I would not let the side down, but I secretly suspected that I would scream for mercy like a coward when the time came. My state of mind was not helped during the next few hours by a continuous stream of Japanese planes, shooting and bombing anything around that moved.

However my father banished our depression with a burst of activity. While he set about lobbying friends and the residents of the Circuit House for a lift to the airfield, we prepared for immediate departure. If George and I looked ridiculous in two shirts and two pairs of shorts, Maisie looked positively insane in three dresses, two pairs of silk stockings and a coat: the baggage restriction had made clowns of us.

Finally, at midday, Father tracked down an officer with a jeep who was prepared to drive us to the airfield regardless of the Japanese fighter planes. As it happened the man's driving was only marginally less frightening than being machine-gunned, and we were saved only by the jeep's ability to keep upright while flying across potholes in the road. But we were grateful for the lift.

At the airfield the officer left us where the low scrub gave way to an expanse of open grassland about a mile long and several hundred yards wide. Our first reaction was dismay, for the runway, which lay in the centre of this open plain, was besieged by a horde of about a thousand refugees. From my eye-level of four foot two inches they looked more like ten thousand. No wonder Colonel Tandon had been eager to get here at dawn.

There seemed no orderly way of securing a seat in a plane. We were told that when a plane landed, a door would be flung open and the first thirty or forty people who managed to scramble in after the wounded would be taken. That left about nine hundred and fifty people still on the runway. Realistically, there was no hope of the five of us forcing our way through this immense human log-jam as a family group.

Yet there was no alternative. We were neatly caught in the rat-trap formed by the mountains around Myitkyina with no way out except by air, and the Japanese army was expected any day. So we stayed. Getting as close as we could to the runway, we lay down in the open under the scorching noonday sun surrounded by our fellow refugees. We had no food, water or shelter, but it was the same for all of us.

Hour after hour we waited but no planes arrived. Nothing crossed the cloudless sky except the white paddy birds, serene and dignified as they flew over us to their feeding grounds by the Irrawaddy. I lay on my back in the rough grass, squinting at the endless blue above me, parched, hungry and frying gently in my many-layered clothes as I silently repeated again and again: 'I wish I could fly away. How I wish I could fly . . .'

Even after the soft pastel shades of evening had settled on the airfield we were still there, gazing listlessly at the sky, listening for the rumble of aeroplanes. But nothing came. Then night fell and gradually clusters of bright stars emerged from the dark heavens.

I watched my parents with a heavy heart, for their disappointment was written on their faces as they roused themselves and set about securing our belongings and sharing out the loads for us to carry.

'Time to go, children,' my father said quietly, as we began the long walk through the empty fields and the burning town, back to the Circuit House.

At dawn next day, even before the Japanese fighter planes had taken to the skies, we were on the move. Packing some bottles of water and the remains of our breakfast into our bags, we set out once more to walk the three miles to the airfield. There were few people about at this hour of the morning but those we met appeared to be going in the same direction. I looked at their bent backs and heavy luggage and decided that when the time came to dive head-long into an open aeroplane door I would beat them hands down. I was feeling light-headed and disorientated and I wondered if I was going out of my mind.

At the airfield we found an immense and agitated crowd milling about near the runway. They were pointing to the hills along the western horizon. Was it an aircraft? By this stage of the war I could identify any military plane by the sound of its engines. But there was no such sound. I scanned the sky again, but there was nothing. Then just as I was about to look away I saw it: a black tubby shape, side-on, two engines, tapered wings, leading-edge swept back, broad tail. Elation surged through me, for before my eyes was a Dakota, banking gracefully, wings outstretched, coming in to land as demurely as a swan.

Suddenly the even-tempered crowd was transformed into an aggressive mob bent on securing a place on the plane. Father heaved George on to his shoulders and ran while Mum sprinted with her longyi lifted up to her knees, her slippers in her hand. Maisie was somewhere, yelling something, but I had gone berserk, butting and pushing people aside as the plane lowered its wheels and touched down.

There was a roar of engines, dust flew in our faces. I could see nothing but feet and backsides ... Hell! I wished I was taller. The crowd surged like a massive tidal wave to

the left, then rolled forward, stopped, flooded forward
again, then swirled to the right as it followed the taxiing
Dakota along the tarmac. I was swept along like a minnow
by the force of this human swell.

Above the heads I could see the propellers spinning,
ready to accelerate the plane for take-off should an enemy
fighter appear. There had been no alarms so far but the
crowd was becoming frantic with anxiety as people fought
to reach the door. Someone stuck an elbow in my back,
while a large woman with two children in her arms smoth-
ered me. I shoved her aside but my right foot was mangled
and I felt my shoulder-bag strangling me. Suddenly the
crush intensified like a giant vice ... They must be opening
the door. Damn! I could not move. I pushed a lumbering
fellow aside, kicked out: 'Come on you swines. MOVE for
goodness sake!' ... I was crushed ... a thought focused in
my head, 'If I lose my footing I'm dead.' I could not breathe.
'Stop pushing you idiot ... this is bloody madness ...
aaahh.' I knew I would be killed in here ... 'Clear off! Go
on clear off. *Shitan! Soower ka batcha! Paggle wallah!*'. My
language was foul.

I thought I was dying ... I cried out, 'Father! Father!
Mum! Mum!' It was no good. There was no sign of my
family. How my head ached ... I yelled to myself, 'Get to
the bloody door' but I could not see it ... only backsides
... just my luck. 'Come on Brookesie, use your elbows ...
go on, hit out! ... again!'

So much dust was being thrown up that it seemed to
pour into my mouth, eyes, nose. It crunched in my teeth
like ground glass. 'What in God's name is happening up
front ... MOVE! COME ON, MOVE IT! ... don't shout

at me you misbegotten son of a cow ... get out of the way.' I tried a kick but it made no difference. Finally I could not move at all. Minutes, maybe hours, were passing by ... I wanted to fly. I wanted to fly away from this nightmare.

The heat and the smell of sweating human bodies was unbearable. Sweat trickled into my eyes but there was nothing I could do about it because my left arm was trapped above my head and my right arm was stuck to my side. I was so worked-up and angry that I felt like screaming. Suddenly, above the clamour of voices, I heard the aeroplane engines roar. There was more dust and the smell of petrol as the crowd began to plunge back and forth in desperation, but I knew I had failed.

My mind was in turmoil. 'Sweet Jesus,' I thought, 'don't let that plane leave without me. Give me a chance. Please.' But I could hear the plane on the runway, the rumble changing into a sustained roar as it gathered speed before easing smoothly into the sky. Above the mass of heads I saw it wheeling in a wide arc, turning into the west wind that would bear it to sanctuary in India.

When the crowd dispersed I fell down where I stood. I had never felt so washed-out. My head seemed to be going round and round and I was terribly scared, but I quickly suppressed the urge to cry in case the others saw me. I was a Brookes and I would never give up. I promised myself that next time I would reach the door and take Mum with me. But now desolation, frustration and rage swept through me, lifting me up then hurling me down. I wanted to swear again but I heard my mother calling my name, so I sat up and tried to look calm.

In a little while our family group was together again, hugging and laughing, soothing brittle nerves and shutting out the misery. Later in the morning we moved to the scrub at the edge of the airfield to find some shelter from the sun. There we feasted on the cold soggy toast and jam and tepid water left over from breakfast. Tired and shaken we lay on the bare earth, locked in uneasy thoughts. Then from the mountains to the west I heard a muffled drone. A minute later I heard it again, more insistent, somewhere in the sky. Again it came, more clearly, a deep, rhythmical 'broom ... broom ... broom'.

I knew that sound – the evocative bass tone of a two-engined plane. It was one I would never forget. I swung round to face the west. There below the high cloud was the sweetest sight – a Dakota of the Royal Air Force cruising gently to earth. Almost immediately the crowd, quiescent since the last episode, erupted.

Sprinting down to the runway on my own I threw myself into the mob, but this time I used my intelligence. Rather than fighting directly towards the door of the plane, I moved round to the right flank and came up from the tail. This meant that my right side was pressed up against the smooth body of the plane leaving only my left exposed to the crowd. I was still boxed in but the awful sensation of drowning in a sea of bodies was lessened. Besides, I could see the open door above their heads, like the entrance to an enchanted grotto.

I caught a glimpse of half-a-dozen stretcher-cases as they were carried along at shoulder height and gently manoeuvred into the plane. Following them came several walking wounded, who were hauled up by two airmen who stood astride the plane door and dragged them in. It occurred to me that these casualties had probably travelled up in the ambulance train with us from Katha three days ago; indeed, they had only got this far because of my father's surgical skills. I was certain that no one there, apart from our family, knew that my father had given these soldiers a chance to live. Now, by an ironic twist of fortune, they were leaving in safety while he was powerless to save his own wife and children.

Eventually the troops on the tarmac who had shielded the wounded moved aside and the refugees made their bid for freedom. Within a couple of seconds I was squeezed like a lemon again. I fought, pushed, kicked and swore. An airman bent down, grabbed a hand, any hand, from the crowd below him and hauled it up, with attached body, into the plane. I waved my hands, but it was fruitless since I did not have thirty-foot arms. Suddenly I heard an awful stomach-churning scream ahead of me: a mother had lifted her child into the plane but before she could follow she was swept aside by the crowd. Things got worse by the second because the airman insisted on taking only women and children, but the husbands were fighting to climb in too. The commotion increased as every refugee shouted for attention and wrestled with those alongside. At this point my nerve finally cracked. I had had enough. It was impossible to move forward so I turned despairingly round and fought my way back to the tail of the aircraft.

The plane was behind me now and the crowd was thinning out a bit. Trembling with fright, sadness, failure and resentment, I looked at the trees and sky and the long empty runway stretching to the horizon. Oh my God! My God! There was a bloody big Dakota landing ... it was slowing down ... stopping ... it turned towards me. 'Sweet Jesus, I'm going to get this one,' I mumbled, 'even if I die in the attempt ... Please God, let it be me.' I started to call out, 'Mum, Father, Maisie, George, run, run.' Damn, where were they? 'Mum! ... MUM! ... MUM!' The mob started running towards the plane. I began to fight and struggle again. 'You bastards, don't push ... Back! Back! ... MUM! Where are you ... MUM! Again the door was opening, I could see it. My thoughts seemed to explode ... 'Fight for it ... Come on ... Fight ... Fight ... Almost there ... Can't breathe ... I'm shaking ... I'm so afraid ... Mum ... MUM! ... MUM! I'm almost there. I've got it! ... JESUS CHRIST I'VE GOT IT!' Both my hands were on the door! 'Hold tight ... Fight them off ... HOLD IT ... Shove them back ... Oh Mum, where are you? ... MUM! ... Don't cry, Brookesie, you're a man ... Oh hell! Help me Jesus ... Somebody help me ...'

I heard a voice above me.

'Come on lad. Hurry.'

It was an airman. He bent down with his arms out-stretched, reaching for me. I looked up and for a moment our eyes met.

'Reach out,' he said.

He looked gentle but I could not move. Something had happened to my body, I felt ice-cold and very tense. I could not stop shivering. The crowd pressed in and began to crush me against the plane but I hung on to the door. The engines were still running, the noise from them and the

My father, William
Lindfield Brookes, as a
28-year-old Assistant
Surgeon in the Indian
army

The Major outside our
home with the bicycle
on which he rode
everywhere

Halcyon days: Mum, Father, Richard and Maisie, Burma, 1924

The Brookes family shortly before the war. *From left to right:*
Janet, Louise, Maisie, Marie;
Richard, Mum, me, Father, George

On the lawn with Maisie

Me and my pups

*(left to right)* George, me and Socksie; in KOYLI kit with my
Daisy air-gun at the ready; young Corporal Brookes with
forage-cap and swagger cane

Pages from
Maisie's diary at
Shingbwiyang.
Since Maisie was
now too ill to
write, I recorded
the doctor's visits

The survivors: Maisie, me, George and
Mum with Maisie's future husband
Jim Whitbread, at Jhansi, India

After the war: me as an 18-year-old
schoolboy at La Martinière College,
Lucknow

crowd beating on my ears like thunder. The airman helped someone else before moving towards me again. 'Hang on. Hang on,' I whispered.

Suddenly a scream exploded in my head, so loud that I could hear it above the other noises. It seemed to detonate deep inside me, leaving me numb and powerless. The feeling was eerie, strange, almost like a hallucination – yet it was real.

The scream in my head said: 'STEVIE! ... DON'T GO! ... STEVIE! ... DON'T GO! ... DON'T GO!'

I turned to face the crowd and there, some distance away, in the centre of the crush, was my mother: her right arm was raised, her hand open, reaching out to me. My father was beside her struggling to restrain her. Her mouth was open, her face white with anguish, her long black hair all dishevelled. She stared at me with dark, wide eyes and from her mouth came this awful scream of pain.

'STEVIE! ... DON'T GO! ... STEVIE! ... DON'T GO!'

My insides started convulsing. It was a waking nightmare. My mother, my family, could not reach me. If I went now, I would go without them. I could not leave – and I did not want to stay.

I don't know how long I held on to the plane door but my fingers were clamped tight and I could not feel them. Through the confusion I heard the airman's voice above me again.

'Are you coming lad? Make up your mind.' But that other call had paralysed me.

Finally the crowd pushed me aside, someone jumped in and the door slammed shut. The engines roared, dust

swirled around me and the plane began to move away. I felt
the tears streaming down my face and I vomited wretch-
edly. I felt completely broken. I'd made it to the door on
my own – yet I could not go, for what would my life be in
a foreign land without my family? They were all I had left.
We had come all this way together. Better to die together
than alone.

'Sorry for frightening you Mum, I'm here now. I will
never leave you. Shhh ... don't cry ... don't cry ...'

Then, in the thick of the noise and confusion, I heard
another voice close to me: 'There's another plane coming
in. Up there! Another plane.'

I looked up and sure enough there was a plane, but I did
not recognise the profile. Then very slowly it banked to the
left and I saw the wings – and on them were two bright red
discs. JAP PLANE! It came down in a steep dive. Jesus
Christ! RUN! ... RUN! ... The plane was coming in
fast . . . I had to get out of the way. The machine-guns
opened up right above me ... missed me, you Jap swine . . .
Christ Almighty! there was another one coming down
behind him, machine-guns firing. Oh shit! ... Sorry God
... RUN! ... RUN! Brookesie ... RUN!

Hundreds of people started fleeing blindly in all directions, abandoning their belongings so they could run faster.
There was bedlam. I tripped over a lost child, someone
barged into me, the noise was deafening. My family was
swallowed up again in this human tidal wave. On a huge
open airfield there was no cover whatsoever. Where should
I run to? Away in the distance I saw the scrub where we
had sheltered that morning. There was no time for second
thoughts for the Jap fighter was coming in again, closing

fast. I began to sprint, twisting this way and that to avoid the other runners. Again a machine-gun opened up in the sky above me and my heart lurched violently.

Somewhere to my right an officer stood still and shouted: 'LIE DOWN! Everybody, lie down. Lie down!'

We all owed our lives to this man, for had we remained upright many of us would have been killed when the bombs exploded. I flattened myself on the open ground just in time as a violent eruption ripped through the air.

I heard someone call 'Stevie!' and looked to my right. It was Maisie about ten yards away, lying flat and facing me. 'Keep your head down, Stevie,' she said.

I tried to smile back. 'I'm OK, Boozie,' I replied. 'Are you all right?'

I looked at the figures on the ground near her but I could not see George. However, in the distance I saw my parents: my father was very calm, his bald head raised as he watched the planes circling us with machine-guns rattling. I supposed he had seen it all before in the First World War and the Afghan War and I wondered if he was actually enjoying this. My mother had her hand on his head and was trying to push it down. I hoped he would not do anything stupid like shooting at them with his pistol because it would have persuaded them to send a few bullets in our direction.

Another bomb went off. When I turned round I realised that the two Dakotas which I had so nearly boarded were hit. Both were still on the runway and from where I lay it looked as though the undercarriage of one had been destroyed, tilting it violently to one side and breaking the wing. The other was on fire and thick black smoke rose high into the sky. Less than fifteen minutes earlier dozens of wounded soldiers, women and children had climbed into these planes to begin a new life in India. But for my mother's intervention I would have been in one of them. I was shaking so much I could hardly speak. 'I'm all right, Boozie,' I mumbled again hoping Maisie could hear me.

The Japanese planes were circling from the runway on my right, across in front of me, then down to my left and behind me to come up to the runway again. They were so low I could see the pilots' faces, yet there was no answering fire from the ground. I knew that a pilot could kill me with a shot to the face as long as I could see him. I could cope with that, but when the plane was behind me the shot would be into my back – and that idea frightened me beyond reason. My back muscles tensed in panic as I waited for the thump of a bullet. 'Will it be very painful?' I wondered. 'Please, please, not the back.'

Suddenly my brain veered out of control and I started to pray very loudly: 'The Lord is my shepherd, I shall not want ... The Lord is my shepherd, He maketh me to lie down in green pastures. Yea, though I walk through the valley of the shadow of death I will fear no evil for Thou art with me. Be near me Jesus ... Forgive me my trespasses before I go ... Boozie, pray! Boozie, pray! ... The Lord is my shepherd ... in the valley of the shadow of death, I shall fear no evil for Thou art with me ... Be with me now ... before I die. No bullets in the back please ... Sorry for everything.'

Then they came again, machine-guns firing on my right. The other plane was behind me firing over the top of us at the Dakotas. I shut my eyes. I did not care any more about being brave. I started blubbering, shivering and praying at the top of my voice and I did not care who saw or heard

83

me. In thirty seconds I could be dead. 'Say it now, say it now' said my mind 'before it is too late ... Our Father ... sob ... who art in heaven, give ... sniff ... give ... Mum, I wish you were next to me ... sob ... I'm scared.'

The firing seemed to go on for ever. Then, abruptly, an uncanny silence fell. We lay where we were, not daring to move or look up. As the seconds ticked by, the realisation that the Jap planes had gone trickled into my numbed mind, but I felt no elation. With dull eyes I looked around. Both Dakotas were wrecks. I could see Mum and Father. Georgie was further away and Maisie was moving. Dried grass and dust stuck to the sweat on our bodies. Mum walked slowly towards us, arms open. We rushed forward, clinging to her fiercely, possessively, revelling in the feeling of being alive. Father was not with us but Mum told us not to worry for, typically, he had rushed off to help the wounded and bury the dead.

When we had recovered sufficiently we made for the airfield perimeter as quickly as our shaky limbs could carry us, and took shelter under some broad-leaved shrubs in a hollow. Hundreds of refugees had dispersed into the scrub and most of them just kept going – wisely, as it turned out, for the fighters returned and shot up the airfield again. This raid was not as terrifying as the first because we were together and some distance away. However, we now began to agonise about Father who was still out on the runway. But an hour later he appeared, striding boldly towards us without the slightest trace of fear.

Our little family group remained in the shelter of the hollow because Japanese air activity was intense. Their fighters swarmed unchecked above the airfield and the town, bombing anything that took their fancy. Yet despite the air-raids we still clung to the faint hope that a Dakota might attempt a landing. The Japanese response to that possibility was not long in coming, for towards evening a bomber appeared over the airfield and blasted the runway. The earth heaved when the heavy bombs went off, signalling what we had always feared: the airfield was now closed for further business. In fact, one Dakota did make a scary landing just before nightfall. We ran down to the runway but before we reached the plane it had hastily scooped up the remaining RAF personnel and departed. That was the last plane out of Myitkyina.

# 6 *Prelude to Disaster*

The last Dakota had gone but still we waited at the airfield. It was a struggle between the will of God and the will of my father. God had decreed that no further planes would land at Myitkyina, a proposition to which my father strongly objected. So he glowered at the darkening sky like a shaman conjuring up aeroplanes. In a way I admired his stubbornness, but frankly the rest of us were exhausted and yearned for soft beds and hot food. Unfortunately when Father was in this mood he was beyond all normal human contact, so we lay on the rough earth and slept while he sweated it out with God.

After half-an-hour he abandoned his solitary vigil and began to collect our belongings for the long trek back to the Circuit House. But it was already too late. The tropical night had fallen and the airfield was plunged in darkness. Somehow we would have to pick our way round the debris and the bomb craters without injuring ourselves; we would also have to find our way through the darkened town where trigger-happy Chinese soldiers awaited the Japanese advance. They had had a bad war and they were itching for easy targets to blast before scampering back to Yunnan. So there was no argument when Father decided we would have to spend the night where we were.

Clinging blindly to one another we shuffled to the airfield perimeter. By chance we stumbled upon a watchman's derelict hut after floundering about in the scrub for several minutes. Bits of the walls and thatch had rotted away while the sagging bamboo floor creaked ominously as we crawled in. There was something dead near-by for there was the reek of decomposing remains, but it was some sort of shelter. We had had nothing to eat since the soggy toast and jam that morning but I was too tired to care. Even the mosquitoes and sand-flies which feasted on us all night could not diminish our sense of good fortune. 'How are the mighty fallen in the midst of the battle. How are the mighty fallen and the weapons of war perished.' The voice of my father reading from the Second Book of Samuel in the Baptist church at home came back to me as I fell asleep.


We rose with the sun and marched resolutely back along the narrow tree-lined road to Myitkyina, glad to be alive and on the move again. Parts of the town were on fire and wrecked and abandoned vehicles littered the fields and grass verges. Japanese fighters circled the dying town, firing on lorries and troops. Each time a plane appeared my family would huddle under a roadside tree or slide into a ditch, making jokes as though all this was perfectly normal. Even lame Georgie played this game. But the trauma of the past few days had brought me to breaking-point and I cowered in terror each time I heard the high-pitched whine of a single-engined Zero fighter.

On a fairly straight section of road we saw a car coming towards us at high speed, the clouds of dust billowing behind it a perfect givaway to any prowling Japanese plane. Sure enough, a dark shape appeared behind it like a hungry shark, streaking down in a tight right-hand turn and coming in fast, heading straight towards us. For a fraction of a second we stood rooted to the spot, then the familiar cry galvanised us into action: 'Run! RUN! RUN! Jap plane.'

As we had just crossed a culvert, we all instinctively dived off the road into the monsoon ditch, plunged through the water and made for the circular concrete pipe-opening under the road. The pipe was just large enough for the five of us to crouch inside: Mum and Maisie with their backs to one wall with Father, George and me opposite. George was the last one in as the plane screeched overhead with machine-guns rattling. The ditch and culvert were raked with bullets which ricocheted off the thick concrete with a shrill *zing* that brought me out in goose-pimples. Some of those bullets had come very close indeed. The note of the engine changed as the plane climbed out of its dive, circling back to make another attempt; but before that, a sudden whine, followed by a long burst of machine-gun fire, told us that the plane had been joined by its mate. Now we knew that a determined attempt was being made to winkle us out of our hiding-place.

At this critical moment we heard a frantic thrashing sound in the ditch as though a stampeding cow was galloping madly through the water towards us. Could it be a Jap?

Five anxious faces stared at the opening and I believe I may have wet myself. Then a figure in a Burmese longyi burst headlong into our refuge, followed immediately by machine-gun fire.

When we had recovered our wits we realised that the stranger who had dropped uninvited into our pipe was a British soldier. In reply to Father's questions he gave an unconvincing story about being in Intelligence, losing his kit and finding a car in which he intended to rejoin his unit. He also said that he had abandoned the car on the road above the culvert to avoid being fired on by the Japanese planes. It now became clear that the planes were attracted to this spot not by us but by the car. I think Father would probably have shot him but for the presence of the family.

I clearly remember hearing its heavy impact on the road before a bomb exploded with an immense roar. The ground shuddered as the blast-wave lashed across the opening of the pipe, followed immediately by the sound of shrapnel pieces crashing through the branches of the over-hanging jungle. The force of the explosion hurled Mum to our side of the pipe where she struck her head violently and slid down in a heap. The rest of us were uninjured, though badly shaken and concussed, and my ears rang with a curious high-pitched whistling sound. It was also difficult to orientate myself in the dust-filled pipe.

We huddled around Mum in the confined space, anx-iously muttering comforting words while Father treated the injury. Fortunately the blow to her forehead was not serious for after a few minutes she responded to our anxious voices with a wan smile. By the time we had eased her out into the fresh air she was her old self again: bossy Mum with a lump on her head, organising her family for the next stage of the journey. But the incident had been deeply unnerving. I had thought she was dead and that black possibility was too harrowing even to contemplate.

We were so engrossed in Mum's condition that it was some time before we realised that the Jap planes had gone, and so too had our mysterious soldier. He would have had to walk, since bits of his car littered the surrounding countryside.

Instead of taking us back to the Circuit House, Father led us to the Civil Hospital, where we were lodged in a small bungalow. George and I were frantic with curiosity. Had Father decided to work in this hospital – regardless of the Japanese presence? Perhaps Mum was to undergo some treatment? But the three adults had become unexpectedly tight-lipped. So as usual we picked on Maisie and through guile and persistence dug nuggets of information out of her.

What we heard was startling but not totally unexpected: Father had decided that he would not run any further. He would work as a surgeon in this hospital, impartially treating the wounded and dying, because it was his profession to save life. I knew Father did not like running because he was an old warrior. But work in this hospital? Japanese planes were machine-gunning the area and the Red Cross flag on the roof seemed only to irritate them and draw their fire. It was madness. From what I had heard, the Japanese were quite capable of bayoneting a doctor, his patients, his wife and family, and I was sure they would not make an exception of us.

But what else could we do? The airfield was closed, and

we had foolishly given up our truck. Added to that we were in the wildest region of Burma, where unbroken primeval jungle cloaked a threatening world of mountains and swamps filled with creatures waiting to maim and kill. We were finished.

The next hour or so is crystal clear in my memory. I can remember exactly where I sat, where I looked, the angle of the sun and even the movements of the family members. It was about six o'clock in the evening and Georgie and I were sitting on the wooden steps of the bungalow. As we looked down the road, our attention was caught by smoke and the sound of gunfire in the distance. The Japanese had arrived. All the doors and windows along the road were shut and there was not a person or a vehicle in sight. The effect was decidedly spooky. It seemed as though there had never been people in the vicinity, yet barely four hours before a crowd of weary refugees had sheltered in the shade of the mango trees by the road.

At that moment I heard an eerie sound floating on the breeze, lingering in the air above the violent sound of the approaching battle. It was like a siren, starting low and ascending gradually to a high-pitched wail. For a few moments I was baffled until I recognised it as the melancholy howl of a dog, a chilling, long drawn-out lament.

I had had enough, and I cried uncontrollably, letting the tears run down my face to spatter my clothes and the wooden steps, while Georgie sniffed softly with his head in his hands. We were expected to sit here calmly and wait to be killed. I was numb with despair.

The three adults were indoors discussing something that excluded us. In a little while Maisie came down the steps and stood beside us. Her eyes were red and it was obvious she was crying. I asked her why and she said quietly: 'Daddy's going to shoot us.'

'*Daddy's going to shoot us.*' They were the most staggering words I had ever heard, yet I remember feeling detached and apathetic. I did not ask why nor did I care. If Father was going to shoot us – so what? I supposed Father would use his pistol so it would be painless. Much better than squealing and snivelling, dishonouring the family name while a Jap butchered me. Maisie sat with us on the step and the three of us wept unrestrainedly because the distant noise of shooting told us that the enemy were getting closer. Either Father or the Japs would decide our fate shortly. Only a miracle could save us.

What happened next was so amazing it defied rational explanation. For out of the smoke, cruising leisurely down the long straight road towards us, like a jolly school bus on an outing, appeared a British army truck with a young soldier at the wheel. There was no one else – no marching troops, no tanks, no convoy – just one truck and a young man getting closer every second. It was incredible, but was it real? My pulse raced and emotion welled up inside me but I could not let go, could not jump up or laugh with relief. Even when the truck drove past us without stopping we did not call or wave. We just sat and watched, dazed by this bewildering shift of events. Had the driver not seen us ... or was this a hallucination? Then, rather dramatically, the brakes were slammed on as though the driver had suddenly registered that it was indeed children he had just seen by the road. He leaned out of the cab window and uttered the immortal words: 'Hey kids! What are you doing there? The Japs are just round that corner. Get in. Hurry.'

Pandemonium! We yelled with relief as we rushed to clamber aboard. By now my parents, realising from the noise that something was afoot, had hurried out of the bungalow. Tempers were frayed and I heard my father insisting that his family must stay in the hospital, while the soldier argued equally insistently that it was a crazy idea and the children should leave with him immediately. Finally he shut the cab door and began to drive off. More arguments. Shots could be heard in the distance. It was now or never. Father wanted to go back for his belongings but the soldier would not wait. He said he would return for them when it was safe, so Father capitulated and climbed in.

We raced out of Myitkyina with the sound of explosions in the distance. Oh, the feeling of deliverance as I held on to my family with trembling hands! My mind raced with joy and relief: 'Yippee, Georgie! Mum, let me kiss the bruises on your forehead. Hi'ya Boozie! Father! We're free: it's a miracle and I'll remember this day for ever and ever amen. Sorry, God, for doubting You. I'm really mixed up because so many things keep changing. Forgive me.'

The unknown soldier drove us out of the town to a bridge about four miles away which he said would be blown up that night. Then he left us, telling my father that he would return with his belongings, but we never saw him again and he passed out of our lives as mysteriously as he had entered them.

Since Father's belongings and the family papers which lay in the bungalow were not retrieved we became true refugees: people without papers, without history, without identity.

It was to take me over half-a-century to come to terms with what I heard that afternoon in May 1942, when Maisie said, 'Daddy's going to shoot us'. Looking back I can understand now that my parents feared my mother and sister might be raped by the Japanese, and had agreed it was better to end our lives while we could still exercise love, compassion and free will.

As a child in Myitkyina I saw the situation differently, but then I knew absolutely nothing about rape or sex – words that were not even in my vocabulary. The thought that our father, a deeply religious and devoted family man, could consider such an option was a massive shock to my psyche. Yet now I understand what torment he must have endured, and pay homage to his courage and humanity.

And so night fell on this extraordinary day. We lay on the bare earth under two blankets which Father had scrounged from a passing military truck. Snuggled safely between Mum and Georgie, I whispered the bedtime prayers that I had always said at Lindfield: 'Gentle Jesus meek and mild, look upon a little child. Pity my simplicity, suffer me to come to Thee ...'

I felt the warmth of my family flooding into me like the sea, driving back the demons of my mind. At about two in the morning we were woken briefly by a tremendous explosion which signalled that the bridge had been blown. On that same day, 8 May, Myitkyina fell to the Japanese army.

To all intents and purposes the battle for Burma was over, though skirmishes continued for a while as the British and

Chinese armies retreated into India and China. There was a sweet irony in what followed, since it was the British Viceroy of India who had wrested Burma from its people in 1886, banishing King Thibaw and Queen Supayalat to exile in India. Now it was the British Governor, Sir Reginald Dorman-Smith, who was exiled to India as Japan grabbed the country for itself. In fifty-six years history had come full circle.

# 7 The Rat Trap

Next day we rose with the sun and joined the mass movement of troops and refugees heading northwards into the unknown. We had become part of the exodus of people driven from their cities by conquerors since the beginning of time. Around us lay the abandoned belongings of the thousands who had gone before us. Broken cars and lorries; mounds of clothing; bags, suitcases and boxes stuffed with the paraphernalia of kitchens, bedrooms and sheds; books and papers in heaps; rusting weapons, piles of ammunition and kit lay strewn in the jungle; and everywhere was the sickly odour of decay.

Rather surprisingly, in view of what we had been through, we were still reasonably dressed, though my dark blue school blazer spouted just a touch of flora and fauna. But my outfit was dull compared to George's high summer fashion-attire of a sola topi with collapsing rim, held together by a shoe-lace tied under his chin. Nevertheless, we happily picked our way through this rubbish, anticipating the day when something as simple as a water-bottle or a box of matches might mean the difference between life or death. Father unearthed a large thermos flask with a capacity of several pints, while I made the best find of the morning – a silver-handled Gurkha kukri. The sword's curved blade was heavily rusted but that did not matter, for it was the power and immense self-confidence the weapon gave me when I strapped it to my belt that was important. From now on I would have the means to defend my family and forage for food.

The road we followed was a wide cart-track cut out of the thick jungle, which rose on either side like a green curtain fifty feet high. Within this gloomy corridor moved a stream of refugees, thousands of them as far as the eye could see – Indians, British, Chinese, Eurasians; troops, civilians, government officials; parents and children, the sick and the dying. There were families pushing barrows laden with children and heavy sacks of food and bedding; bullock carts swaying with the weight of people crowded on their flimsy frames; lorries, cars, bicycles, army trucks, jeeps, cattle and the occasional elephant – all loaded to breaking point with people and belongings. And entwined in this curious procession were thousands more on foot: plodding, sleeping, cooking, giving birth and dying in the jungle. Our family was a mere grain of sand in this dust-storm.

Full of excitement and determination, we were loaded up and moving across the Myitkyina plain like racehorses on the loose at six o'clock that morning. Even lame Georgie seemed to have experienced a miracle cure as he strode out effortlessly with the adults, shouting the occasional insult at me.

'Keep up Stevie! Do you want me to carry you, you big baby?'

During this first day of serious trekking we covered a blistering twelve miles with barely a pause, before subsiding in a sweaty heap beside a stream late in the afternoon. All day the others were fired up and bursting with energy but I felt tired and irritated, especially since the Gurkha kukri hanging on my belt kept stabbing me in the calf as I walked – a problem I eventually solved by strapping it across my back. However, I was still daunted by the speed at which we were moving and I made a silent wish, God forgive me, that someone, preferably Maisie, would be blessed with a twisted ankle before too long.

I was unexpectedly saved by a truck brim-full with refugees which lumbered into view. At my insistence Father spoke to the driver, money changed hands, and in a trice a sliver of space was found in the back for the five of us. It was cramped, but a thousand times better than walking. Through the rest of the evening and night the overburdened vehicle inched its way forward in a cloud of fumes, both human and vehicular, till we reached a dak bungalow ten miles further on.

I expected Father to settle here for the night, but he was in one of his inscrutable moods again and decided we would continue our trek, although it was now midnight and pitch black. There was no sense in this, but sense had deserted us over a month before, so we followed him dutifully in the dark, cursing him silently for his stubborness. He had led us no more than a few miles when a lorry appeared behind us, and with one accord we abandoned any semblance of family solidarity and eagerly waved the driver to a halt. We clambered in with Father last, growling like a scalded tom-cat at our lack of stamina. Finally, at 4 a.m., after bumping and rattling along the uneven jungle track for ten awful miles, the lorry stopped by a suspension bridge. Numb with exhaustion we staggered out, laid our aching bodies on the bare earth and fell asleep instantly.

Though Father was elated with our magnificent dash of thirty-two miles in twenty-two hours my own joy next morning was muted, for my feet were raw with blisters and my back ached unmercifully. However, it was certainly an excellent start. The Japanese patrols would have to hurry if they were to stand a chance of catching us.

That day we put in another brisk eighteen miles and spent the night beside a bridge. Bridges began to have special significance for us refugees, for they allowed us to cross rivers without getting drowned, and indicated the presence of precious water for cooking and washing. The daily stage of a trek, I soon learned, was from one stream to another – which was fun when the next stream was eight miles away but purgatory when it was eighteen, for my legs were short and I had a load to carry. Failure to reach a watering-hole meant a revolting dinner of stale rice shared between the five of us.

We were now at the head-waters of the Irrawaddy, a thousand miles from its mouth in the Bay of Bengal. Below us the current swirled around rocky outcrops where the Irrawaddy's tributaries, the Mali Hka and the Namai Hka, met for the first time on their journey from the high mountains on the Burmese border with Tibet and China, three hundred miles to the north. It was in this region, near the snow-covered peaks of Hkakabo Razi, over 19,000 feet high, that the deluge of monsoon rain and melting snows mixed to create this mighty river. For the first time I realised that we were a long, long way from home.

My father, who was still in his uniform complete with solar topee, Sam Browne belt and handy pistol, was probably using his influence at this stage of our journey, because next day we secured another lift to a dak bungalow ten miles away. The road was getting steeper for we had entered the foothills of the Kumon range, a southern spur of the Himalayas which separates the Hukawng Valley, where the Chindwin river rises, from the head-waters of the Irrawaddy. This daunting barrier, made up of precipitous jungle-clad ridges and deep valleys, ended in a peak almost 8,000 feet high within twenty-five miles of Myitkyina. The bare earth road now had an ominous look, quite unlike its friendly aspect in the plains. Steep inclines with vertical drops on one side alternated with twisting hairpin bends and landslides. Abandoned vehicles in the jungle and wrecks at the foot of the cliffs warned us of the dangers of this section of our escape route.

During the night we were on the move again, but progress was slow. The driver, who smoked a vile brand of cigarettes, was skilled, but after a couple of brushes with disaster even he felt it was unwise to continue. Once again we slept on the ground by the roadside. In the morning we decided to walk the remaining few miles to the next dak bungalow, which we reached without mishap. Here we rested and spent the night in relative comfort.

On 12 May 1942 the monsoon began. General Slim, the Commander of 1 Burma Corps, observed that it nearly destroyed the British army. But it also stopped the Japanese dead in their tracks. It was simply our bad luck that this area of Burma, which shares a border with Assam, has an average annual rainfall of over 100 inches.

While this might not have been dramatic on the open plains, it was a very different thing among the ridges of the Kumon range. The rain-water saturated the thick jungle and cascaded down the mountain slopes in a brown slurry which obliterated roads and turned footpaths into knee-deep quagmires of thick gooey mud. What had once been tiny streams thundered past in terrifying flash floods, and benign rivers became barriers of deep swirling water that ripped and smashed trees in their path. The flood-waters that could not drain away drowned the valleys, turning them into vast swamps where malarial mosquitoes, midges, snakes and leeches multiplied.

Meanwhile, in the jungle the humidity rose to over 80 per cent and the temperature soared to 90 degrees Fahrenheit. In this hothouse nothing grew, nothing lived that did not prey on its neighbour in the fight for survival. No one entered this domain during the south-west monsoon without an abnormal reason for doing so.

We left the bungalow by truck at 10.30 a.m. with the rain coming down in sheets, so it was hardly surprising that we ran into trouble before we had travelled very far. The day before the road had been dry and firm but now it was a treacherous skating-rink of churned-up brown slush in which the wheels of our lorry skidded and spun out of control. Negotiating the hairpin bends on the steep inclines was now very hazardous because it was impossible for the driver to take the curve in one sweep. Instead, he had to make a series of heart-stopping forward and reverse moves until he had inched the vehicle past the bend and entered the straight section of the incline.

Our small problem arose when the driver, who had successfully inched his way round a hairpin bend, braked as he was carrying out the final reverse. The fickle tyres buried in the slush could not hold the weight of the lorry, and it slid backwards down the incline towards the crumbling edge. In a trice the off-side rear wheel went over the cliff and the lorry tilted over, hurling a refugee who was standing at the back into the abyss. Had the rear chassis not sunk into the verge, instantly stopping our slide to death, this book would not have been written. However, we were left dangling in space at an alarming angle. I remember so clearly the way the lorry rocked from side to side over the void, while the occupants struggled to cling on to something to stop themselves sliding out. Everyone screamed the single message: 'Stay still! Everybody, stay still! Don't move!'

I just had time to grab Mum's leg as the lorry tilted, but it was a precarious hold on life. Yet every effort I made to improve my position provoked a crescendo of voices.

'Don't move. Do you want us to die?'

After about half-an-hour another lorry, crammed with passengers, slid to a halt behind us. Grappling ropes were tied from our lorry to trees across the road, stabilising our position. Finally we were roped to two lorries and dragged, slithering, up the incline to a chorus of muffled screams from the passengers.

'Dear God!' I thought. 'Is this some kind of test of faith? Kill us or save us, but stop messing about please.'

Before we resumed our journey, Father and a couple of

men climbed down to the man who had been thrown out, but there was nothing they could do for him. He had probably died instantly when he hit the ground, so they left him there at the foot of the cliff in the pouring rain. On this harrowing exodus, I realised, there was no strength, no means, and no obligation to bury the dead. You lay where you fell. Best not to think it could happen to anyone in our family.

When at last we reached a dak bungalow we stopped to rest and compose ourselves before continuing our journey later that evening. It was pitch black and very dangerous, but we were impatient to be gone and we paid the price. In the darkness the lorry skidded and veered off the road once again. We were saved this time by the fortuitous presence of a tree on the verge which held us, but Father fell out of the lorry and disappeared from sight.

'Willie! Willie! Say something, Willie.'

Mum was in such a state that we thought she was going to slide down the cliff to help him, so we grabbed her, adding our voices to the general uproar.

'Father! Daddy! Where are you? Are you hurt?'

To our astonishment an irritated voice no more than six feet below us replied: 'Do stop that noise, children. Calm down, everyone. I'm on my way up.'

With much huffing and puffing my father scrambled up the slope, great dollops of red mud trickling off his uniform as he approached the stranded vehicle. I grinned in the darkness when I heard him muttering under his breath as he scraped the sludge off with a twig.

Meanwhile a passing lorry-driver kindly helped us by hitching a tow-rope to our stricken transport and dragging it away from the tree. By now we were becoming inured to such disasters so we continued on our way, stopping only when we reached the next dak bungalow. It was dark and silent, so we lay down on the floor of the truck and slept, totally exhausted.

We had come to a halt on the evening of 14 May, having covered twenty-four miles in two days, when we heard the sudden roar of a low-flying aircraft directly overhead. Refugees scattered in all directions so I sprinted deep into the jungle, diving headlong into a thick clump of bamboo and burrowing down like a rabbit. Bamboo scales are covered in a thick layer of sharp black hairs which penetrate the skin and break off, leaving the victim with a layer of inflamed blisters and an agonising rash. When I ran back to the truck for sympathy Father had nothing to give me except quinine and iodine. I itched and *itched* for days.

Thank heaven Father did not have his full surgical kit with him because he loved cutting things: anything from lancing a boil to complete amputations. I think he believed that the road to salvation was through pain – lots of it – and that anaesthetics, which were invented by weaklings, impaired the human spirit. His speciality was to operate on himself, with me watching in horror, to remove lead pellets which had worked their way to the surface of his skin from old shot-gun wounds.

The place where we stopped was known as Milepost 102. Ahead of us the track wound up the hills for forty miles to a tiny settlement called Sumprabum, or 'Mountain of Mists'. It stood on a ridge 3,700 feet above the river valley of the Mali Hka, along a cart-track which led on to the lonely outpost of Fort Hertz. Beyond lay a wilderness of mountain ridges, deep gorges, impassable streams, snow-covered peaks, Tibet and China.

We had reached the end of the cul-de-sac and the mountains had closed in. Apart from some bungalows and barracks for a detachment of Frontier Force troops, plus some Indian and Chinese shops and Kachin huts, there was nothing at Sumprabum. Dark rain clouds and thick mist enveloped the area for six months of the year. Try as one might, it was difficult to find any redeeming features to it as a place of sanctuary.

Other refugees had reached the same conclusion, for the glade around Milepost 102 was littered with the abandoned debris of their passing. It was a graveyard for all mechanical means of transport and the jungle had already begun to claim scores of rusty skeletons. From here on, the only means of movement would be feet: human, cattle or elephant. We sat down on the wet grass amongst hundreds of tired and anxious people, all thoroughly soaked by the torrent of monsoon rain, all desperately hoping that their next decision would be the right one.

When, in a short time, my father returned from his discussions with the other refugees, a glance at his grim face warned me that he was about to tell us something unpleasant. I was right. While we huddled around him, Father rehearsed the reasons why we should not continue our journey to Sumprabum and why returning to Myitkyina was not an option. Then he paused, as though trying to find the right form of words. I remember sitting very still, staring at the ground. I was scared to look up at my father and scared of what was coming next. When he spoke again his voice was gentle, rather sad.

'We have only one hope,' he said. 'And that is to walk westwards through the jungle, climb the Kumon range to the Daru pass, then trek through the Hukawng Valley and over the Patkoi range and the Pangsau pass until we reach India.'

I could not believe my ears. But worse was to come.

He told us that it would be a horrifying trek, worse than anything we had experienced so far, and that we would suffer terribly. But we would be together as a family, helping each other, supporting each other. We were in God's hands and we must not lose faith. Then Father said something that made me go quite cold.

'Tomorrow morning we will set out to walk the three hundred miles to India.'

My mind did a couple of wild whirls and I wondered if I had heard him correctly. What did he mean: walk three hundred miles to India? We had no clothes except those on our backs; we were carrying some cooking utensils, rice, coarse flour, water, milk powder and two blankets. That was all. No tent, no groundsheet, no waterproof clothing. It was like leaving Lindfield all over again but that had been a civilised affair in comparison. This was going to be a mission through hell. Even as a child I realised that following a trail through dense jungles and swamps, across mountains and rivers for three hundred miles in the rainy season was an impossible venture. Surely my father was wrong. But he went on to tell us that for a payment of one hundred rupees, a Gurkha had agreed that we could join his group. They would share their food with us and allow us to put some of our belongings on one of his bulls. That was it.

I remember how Mum and Maisie stared impassively at their feet and even Georgie seemed unmoved. Perhaps stunned would be a better description. I had a very bad feeling about the whole expedition, but I was too inarticulate, too nervous to speak up. What could I, a mere 11-year-old, say? As far back as I could remember, every facet of my life had been governed by 'duty' – to God, King and Country; to my parents and my family; to my school, the Church, our servants. We were the last of the Empire's children, fashioned for a world of certainties but living in a world in transition. What an awful, frightening mess. I put my hands up to hide my eyes because I knew that men did not cry. But oh God, how I cried inwardly.

Whether we would have gone if we had known the facts is debatable. The first barrier which lay across our path was the Kumon range, steep parallel ridges up to 4,000 feet high and covered by some of the densest jungle in Burma. During the monsoon hundreds of streams meandered down the ridges and these would have to be crossed and re-crossed several times in a single hour as the trail descended in long loops to the bottom of one ridge, only to rise in ascending loops up the next.

Beyond this was a vast valley over a hundred miles wide, awash with rivers and swamps under an unbroken canopy of primeval jungle. It appeared on maps as the Hukawng Valley but had also become known before the war as the 'Valley of Death' on account of a massacre of the inhabitants by the Naga headhunters who dwelt in the hills above. Through the swamps flowed rivers which could only be crossed by rafts tied to pulleys on the far bank, while the humid jungle bred cholera, dysentery, malaria, jungle sores, typhoid and a myriad other sicknesses.

Beyond the Hukawng Valley rose another range of hills, the Patkoi range, as wild and steep as the Kumon range and also interlaced with rivers. In a fold of the hills 4,000 feet above the valley lay the Pangsau pass from which the trail led eastwards to India.

By any stretch of the imagination, the task of walking across these obstacles during the monsoon would have seemed impossible. But in May 1942 we knew nothing of what lay ahead of us. So we mingled with the other exiles at Milepost 102, sharing their camaraderie. The hard decision had been made and tomorrow we were off to India.

Late that evening we moved in with the Gurkha party as they were about to dine. They were gathered round a smouldering fire of wet logs on which two large aluminium pots simmered with enough hot rice and potato curry to make a starving boy swoon. We were each given a piece of banana leaf for a plate and shown to our allotted space on the wet grass with the decorum of a maître d'hôtel leading us to our reserved tables at the Ritz. Greetings of '*Salaam Sahib, baithiye*', '*Aiye Memsahib, khanna kaiye*', '*Chullo Baccha*' punctuated our passing. Being the youngest, I drew the short straw as usual and was seated next to a cross-eyed bull which nudged me and dripped wet stuff from its mouth on my shirt all evening. But I remember vividly the delicious taste, the aroma, even the texture of the food.

At last night fell on the gathering at Milepost 102.

Parents, children, friends and fellow travellers huddled close to each other by the embers of their fires. The grass was cold but the indomitable spirit of these people fuelled a sense of solidarity that filled us with courage.

# 8  *Racing the Monsoon*

My brother and I rolled out of the saturated wallow in which we had slept, like a couple of baby water-buffaloes greeting the dawn. A number of leeches, still clinging to our bodies though gorged and swollen with blood, were quickly dispatched with flicks from my kukri. But Mum disapproved of this, preferring to let the creatures drop off naturally when they were ready.

In truth, what with my father's wild God of Hell and Damnation and my Asian mother's gentle words on the sanctity and oneness of all life-forms on the Eternal Wheel of Life, I was forever shuttling between the two extremes. Perhaps my parents' attempts to guide me were causing me more confusion than illumination.

At last, the caravan in the meadow transformed itself into a continuous line of fugitives: civilians, soldiers, women, children, the strong and the weak, all burdened with loads they could scarcely carry. They shuffled forwards in their pathetic little groups to the point where the track disappeared through a dark gap in a wall of unbroken jungle sixty feet high.

Somewhere in the midst of this ragged throng walked the Brookes family. I remember desperately trying to assume an air of bravado, although my heart was pounding with fright at the thought of the unknown dangers ahead. Leading our little tribe was Father, still brisk and smart in his army uniform, carrying the flask of boiled water and on his back a heavy army haversack in which he had secreted his pistol.

Clutching the strap of the haversack was George, his unsteady feet forcing him to lean so heavily on this support that the strap cut into Father's back. Georgie was a hero with amazing courage. He shuffled across logs on raging rivers and limped up mountainsides without a whimper of fear, and was as strong-willed and bloody-minded as our parents.

Mum walked behind them. Once she would have been decked out with jewels, garlands of flowers and a hair-comb of gold, but to-day she was plain and unobtrusive, a grey shadow meekly following her husband. On her shoulder was a patterned Shan bag bulging with the necessities for her hungry brood, while on her head she balanced what looked like a knotted shawl of swag.

I did not understand until years later that Mum and Maisie had intentionally made themselves look scruffy in order to avoid the attentions of the male predators who roamed the jungle. It had never occurred to me that as well as struggling desperately with the elements, disease and starvation, we would also have to guard against attacks by other human beings.

Next in line came Maisie, my brittle-nerved sister, who

invariably screamed when faced with mice, storms, dark rooms, injections, dogs, ghosts, bats, things that banged, things that squeaked, and things that did neither. She would jump at the movement of her own shadow. From my earliest memory her call rings out: 'Oh my God! Stevie, what's that scratching sound? Have a look, I'm scared. Stevie, what's that black thing in the dark? Hold my hand.'

She carried a bag of personal belongings on her back, gripping it like an octopus for she knew my sense of humour. I had once tried to introduce her to a friendly grass snake and it had almost pushed her over the edge. She still shied away from anything that looked as if it might wriggle.

I came last, still neatly dressed for school, though my clothes were dripping with rain-water. On my belt was my silver-handled kukri and in my hand a large container of malted milk powder. For some reason I also carried a heavy set of keys in my trouser pocket, the key-ring attached to my belt by a silver chain. My blazer pockets were stuffed with treasures from my secret chest at Lindfield: handfuls of coloured stones, bits of rusting metal which might turn out to be gold, and a damp photo of my dead brother Richard. I also carried string, wire, coins, screws and nails, a few genuine uncut Burmese rubies, bits of coloured glass, a magnifying glass, bullets for a .303 rifle, pins, bull's-eye sweets, a small penknife and a pencil stub.

My role in the family regiment was to act as the rearguard: in other words, the first to be eaten when a tiger jumped out of the jungle behind us, and the last to run when those in front fled without warning. They called me 'Brave Stevie' to soothe their consciences. But small though

I was, I was growing in confidence and tenacity each day, for my survival instincts were being honed with each crisis.

On this damp May morning, our bizarre-looking family group set off to scale the track that wound up the first ridge of the Kumon range. A week before, it would have been dry and firm and the going would have been easy, but unfortunately for us the monsoon had started before we could get away.

Conditions were made worse by the thousands of people ahead of us who had trampled the steep sides into a deep porridge. Two steps up, slide down one. Up again. Down again. Shuffle sideways, holding on to a protruding root for safety while the right foot moves carefully through the porridge to find a firm toe-hold. Get a grip, move again. After an exhausting climb we had barely covered a mile. But if a thousand other people could do it, the Brookes family could do it too, I had no doubt about that.

'Come on, keep moving sister.'

'Oh, do shut up, Stevie. Something wriggled under my foot.'

'You're in luck.'

'Mummy, this child is annoying me again.'

As we climbed, the wind increased in intensity and the overcast sky began to give way to a billowing mass of thick black clouds. Driven northwards by the strong south-west wind, this wall of racing clouds crashed into the mountain-sides like icebergs hitting land, spewing out pent-up water that fell to earth in sheets of blinding rain. Within seconds we were drenched to the skin. The temperature dipped and the light began to fade although it was scarcely noon. Brilliant flashes of lightning streaked through the clouds.

Below us the valleys echoed to the deep-throated rumble of thunder that shook the ground we stood on.

The track started to flow away, becoming soft and very dangerous. Even to transfer the weight of the body from one foot to the other without proper preparation was lethal. My attention was totally focused on the problem and every nerve tingled; muscles tensed, ready to respond immediately to a fall. I glanced at the slope below us as we inched forward, marking the trees in my memory so that I could grab one on the way down if I slipped. We all breathed deeply – no one spoke. Occasionally, when someone up front managed to get a firm hold on something solid, hands would stretch out to link the rest of us together and we would move forward like a human caterpillar.

I could not imagine how Father was struggling up this slope with Georgie hanging on to him. Wisps of mist drifted past and I sometimes lost sight of him, but I could make out Mum and Maisie just ahead of me with their bundles. My kukri was stabbing me in the leg again but this was not the place to let go and fasten it to my back. The big tin of malted milk was also causing me major problems. It was too heavy and awkward to drape round my neck or shoulder so I held it by the handle: this meant that I had only one hand left to grab at passing roots and tufts of grass. To bolster my courage I whispered the injunction my brother-in-law from the King's Royal Rifles used to utter when I was too boisterous at home: 'Steady the Buffs! Steady the Buffs!'

On we climbed, following the treacherous path higher and higher, each move precisely determined. Hold-balance-move. Hold-balance-move. Once we got the rhythm it was not too frightening. Sometimes, when it was safe to, I would rest and look back at the section we had climbed. I wished I had a camera, for clambering up the watery slope behind us was a long line of people in much the same state as ourselves.

Our Gurkha friends were behind us in a group led by their Sergeant or Havildar. He and another man were in charge of the two bulls carrying the rice and heavier baggage. I could not bear to watch their dangerous ascent as they heaved on the bull's halter with one hand while applying a stick to its back with the other.

By midday we had reached the crest of the ridge, and began the equally terrifying descent. The only safe way of making progress now was to lean back, plant one foot securely, bend the knee, then gingerly slide the other foot forward to a secure base before repeating the manoeuvre. The sound of the Gurkha's bull slithering down the slope behind me was so unnerving that in my haste I nearly collided with those in front.

Eventually we reached the base of the ridge, but before we could start up the next we had to cross a stream. It was waist-deep and hardly a dozen yards wide, but the strength of the current was formidable, and I was terrified when one of my feet was swept from under me while the other began to slide downstream before I could regain my balance. I tried to think of the scratchy black-and-white films of Johnny Weissmuller, the Tarzan of my youth, swimming fearlessly through crocodile-infested rivers to rescue Jane — but it was no good, for I could not swim.

The only safe way to cross these streams was for a group of people to link hands, hold very tight, and inch purposefully across. Keeping one's nerve was crucial, for even if the water was chest-high – which it usually was for me – it was still safe to cross as long as the chain of hands remained unbroken. Holding Maisie's hand in these circumstances was frightening for it was all I could do to stop her letting go of my hand in mid-stream. I was also scared witless at having to immerse myself in black water with unseen things grabbing at my bare feet in the deep ooze. But I held on and kept my mouth shut – unlike my sister, who screamed at every crossing: 'Aaaaa! there's something biting me. Stevie, I can't hold on, I'm going to let go. Help! Help! I'm drowning. Mum. Mum. I'm drifting away. Stevie! Stevie! My hand's slipping.'

Despite the continuous rain we climbed to the top of the next ridge but on the way down our spirits began to droop. The track had deteriorated dangerously and there seemed to be an unspoken communal agreement that we could go no further. So, by silent consent, the winding trail of refugees left the track for an outcrop of open jungle and made camp for the night.

It was difficult to get the fires going, but with persistence they were kept burning long enough for the wonderful aroma of cooked food to drift through the camp. At Lindfield we had been taught to respect food and the person who cooked it and to thank God who provided it: so we said our grace and ate our meal quietly and thoughtfully, even though our plates were banana leaves and the cutlery was our fingers.

Then came the best part of the day – the time to rest and sleep. What a blessing it was to lie between Georgie and Boozie on the wet mud under a wet blanket which we shared with leeches and mosquitoes. Drifting in the dark, all fears and pains fading, I felt waves of peace flow gently through my mind and body.

> Jesus tender shepherd hear me
> Bless thy little lamb to-night.
> Through the darkness be thou near me
> Watch my sleep till morning light.

We had trekked seven miles that day. Considering the terrain and the dreadful weather it was not a bad start. Perhaps things would look better in the morning.

In fact they looked worse. There was so much water stagnating on the ground we could well have drowned while we slept. However we set off downhill at a reasonable pace with my father in the lead humming a rumbustious Baptist hymn to restore our flagging spirits.

It was at this point on the trek that I discovered the fundamental principle of survival under monsoon conditions. The secret, as every wild animal knows, is not to treat the rain as an opponent. Fighting the monsoon led to exhaustion – whilst trying to keep dry led to insanity. The answer was calm acceptance. It was as simple as that.

So I went slippie-sliding my way to India like a contented water rat. Behind me the Gurkhas were alternately pulling on the bulls to stop them sliding downhill and whacking them with sticks to make them move forward. It made no sense to the bulls. All of a sudden one of them lost its temper. With a wild bellow which had me and the Gurkhas scampering for the safety of the trees, it plunged off the path and down the steep mountainside. Blankets, pots and pans, rice and everything else clattered down with it. The poor beast crashed into trees, its four legs waving wildly while it swung its head violently from side to side like a matador's prize bull. It extricated itself with a bellow and fell further into the jungle, then, with a final roar that probably meant 'I've had it,' disappeared into the undergrowth. There was a clatter of hooves for a few seconds – then silence. The entry in Maisie's small diary was laconic: 'One bull did the bunk with our blankets.'

The people on the hillside stood motionless, shocked by the drama of a bull going manic. I guess there was also a sneaking feeling of envy because we all felt like running away, galloping headlong over the cliff to freedom. But we were human beings with a sense of responsibility, so we stood still and suffered in silence.

The Gurkhas seemed genuinely mystified by the animal's bizarre behaviour. They stared morosely down the steep hillside, mumbling among themselves in Gurkhali. Then to cries of '*Chullo! Chullo!*' they continued down the track with the one remaining bull. Now we had less of everything and the same number of people to feed and shelter.

Disappointed but defiant, we plodded along to the next ridge until we came to a point where further trekking was clearly out of the question. Great tracts of the jungle were under water, and the path had disappeared. Worse still, the water concealed deep potholes and gullies, and my usual sense of humour deserted me after my second ducking. The others found it amusing to see me frantically doggie-paddling while holding the tin of milk powder aloft. But then, they were several feet taller than me.

To our relief we came across four abandoned Kachin huts in a clearing. They were all derelict, the residents having bolted into the jungle on the arrival of thousands of diseased refugees. Luckily the one we commandeered had a bamboo floor and bits of thatch roofing which gave us some protection, and Father soon put my kukri to good use chopping down broad-leaved bushes and branches which we used to construct a more efficient roof. I really enjoyed this because it reminded me of the fun we used to have at the Anisakan Scout Camp beside the river near Maymyo called Laughing Waters.

We were trapped here for a day and a half by the rain, which was so dense that just standing in the open made you feel as if you were drowning. However we still had to forage for food from the jungle to supplement what we were carrying. Here my mother's knowledge of edible and poisonous plants was invaluable, and under her supervision we became experts at collecting leaves for supper.

I had gone out in search of bamboo shoots for the 'duty chef', a wizened Gurkha lady who used to squat patiently beside the miserly flames of her fire, blowing her nose and stirring the rice with the same hand. I had strayed into the thick undergrowth a short distance from the camp when I became aware of an unusual smell. Moving cautiously round the base of a bamboo clump with my kukri in my hand, I approached a tree-trunk which lay across my path.

As I stepped over it a huge black cloud of flies rose up in front of me and a foul stench hit my nostrils. Before I could prepare myself, my eyes had taken in the awful sight of a bloated brown thing covered in a thick mass of wriggling white maggots. It had once been a human being, but now it looked like any decomposing animal. The distended belly heaved and moved with insects; stiff mouldy limbs stuck up through the weeds, glistening with black flies.

During the weeks and months ahead I was to see hundreds of dead and dying people. I walked over them and sometimes, too exhausted to move, I slept next to them. I saw the dead in grotesque postures, rotting in the mud, the rivers and the jungle. I saw them in ones and piled up in dozens; in family groups and in whole camps. In the end, I became inured to the process of death. But I never forgot the first corpse I saw at close quarters, when I was a child, alone in the jungle.

As the years went by, this indelible memory destroyed the fragile belief that a spirit could possibly reside in that rotting flesh. Those whose picture of death is of a well-made wooden box in a grave lined with flowers do not know how fortunate they are, for they can sing 'Abide with me' without the memory of the smell and the maggots blotting out the words.

# 9  *The Butterflies of Kumon*

O ur dilapidated shelter began to crumble under the continuous pounding of wind and rain. Finally, when our attempts to shore up the roof with bamboo poles failed yet again, we knew it was time to go.

Another worry was the precarious state of our food supplies. The Gurkhas had set out with enough rice to feed the group for two weeks which, barring accidents, would have been sufficient to take us over the Kumon range to the edge of the Hukawng Valley. But the bull had scattered most of this rice on the hillside as it plunged down the ridge. It was clear that, irrespective of conditions, we would have to keep moving to find another source of food.

Filled with foreboding we left the huts and moved on through the jungle. The entry in Maisie's diary for 19 May describes our trek of seven miles as tedious and very slushy. What the adults did not seem to realise was that I was almost up to my thighs in thick gooey mud, and not waving but drowning. It gripped my shoes and wrenched them off my feet at every step. Tying my laces tighter made no difference and having to shove my arm repeatedly into the ooze to search for the missing shoes was exhausting. Occasionally, someone would look back and yell through the jungle: 'Come on Stevie, stop playing in the mud. Keep up or the tigers will get you.'

Fortunately they were too far away to hear my reply.

Finally I did the obvious thing and left my socks and shoes embedded in the slush for ever. The effect was spectacular: I was like a fly freed from a sticky fly-paper. On nimble bare feet I scampered after the others, making up a fanciful story to explain to my mother how my best shoes came to be missing. Imagine my disgust when I caught up with them and found that they had *all* thrown their shoes away. No wonder they found the going merely 'tedious' while I had found it life-threatening.

Even so I was certain that the loss of our shoes was very serious, for between us and India stretched almost three hundred miles of undergrowth bristling with thorns, stings, sharp edges and biting insects. From now on we would have to face these in our bare feet. Woe betide anyone who got a cut sole or an infected jungle sore, for the ability to keep moving was crucial. Those who stopped, died.

Shortly afterwards we paused for a short break in an open stretch of jungle. Freed from the tangle of trees and creepers, we had superb views of the ridges which barred our way to India, their green crests rolling away from us like an ocean. We sat on a log, staring at the view, lost in a private world of doubt and fear.

Now a curious incident took place that has reverberated in the dark tunnels of my mind for the past half century.

My father drew a small leather-covered copy of the New Testament from his shirt pocket. For a few moments he flicked through it until he came to what he was looking for. Then he passed it to me. It was open at 1 Corinthians, chapter 13.

'Son,' he said. 'I want you to read a few verses of that chapter each day and memorise them. Repeat them to me every evening until you can recite the whole of it by heart. Will you do that for me?'

I was bewildered, wondering if my Old Man was becoming unstable under the strain. This was hardly the moment for a test in religious knowledge. Surely the priority was to survive. My school exams could come later, assuming I was still alive to sit them. Besides, the chapter had thirteen verses, which was much more than I had ever memorised. But it was a challenge and I could not resist it.

As convincingly as I could I replied: 'All right Father, I'll do it.'

He reached out and put his hand on my shoulder. His grip was strong and reassuring, and I had a distinct feeling that he was trying to communicate something of importance to me. He looked at me quizzically for a long time, then left.

I sat stroking the delicate pages of damp paper as the words flooded into my consciousness, like the half-forgotten lyrics of a song:

Though I speak with the tongues of men and of angels, and have not charity, I am become as sounding brass, or a tinkling cymbal.

And though I have the gift of prophecy, and understand all mysteries, and all knowledge; and though I have all faith; so that I could remove mountains; and have not charity, I am nothing . . .

. . . And now abideth faith, hope, charity, these three; but the greatest of these is charity.

In the beginning the verses meant little to me – they were just bewildering words which I recited to my father each day. But much later, I discovered that there were many strands in his message to me, the greatest of them being his plea to hold on to love – 'charity' – despite the spiritual wilderness that awaited us.

Later that day we found shelter in a derelict Kachin hut which we stumbled upon while trying to find a way round a landslip. The whole structure sagged to one side, probably the effect of the recent storms, but it was reasonably dry inside so we moved in. Meanwhile the Gurkhas, who had been scavenging in the area for food, discovered a discarded bag of rice which they transformed into a superb one-course dinner. Starvation was miraculously changing my perception of food, for in the golden days at Lindfield I would never have believed that plain boiled rice could be so delicious.

It was during this infernal deluge that I invented a unique multi-purpose vegetable umbrella. It was cheap and fashionable, with the added advantage that you could use it as a plate. Moreover, if you were so inclined, you could probably eat the plate as well. The technical details were quite straightforward. First find a banana tree. Then lop off one of the leaves, which in tropical jungles grow to about six feet long. Bend the central rib back approximately two feet from the end, and hold the leaf over your head. The effect was magical, for the front two feet protected your chest while behind you trailed four feet of friendly waterproof leaf covering your back. However, I must admit that although a few refugees were seen using this outstanding invention in 1942, the vast majority preferred to get wet.

Finally on the third day, with food stocks running low, we made a desperate run through the rain to the next deserted Kachin village seven miles further down the track. Although some of the ground water was draining away at the head of the valley, where we were it was still rising and the forest floor began to look like a vast lake. The flooded landscape was a daunting sight and a good reason to remain where we were, but we knew we must get as far down the track towards India as possible before we were cut off by the rising rivers.

For two days we sheltered in a hut, pounded ceaselessly by the rain. Finally, on the afternoon of 25 May, the decision was taken to quit the village as we had run out of food. Plunging boldly into the water, we waded for eight preposterous miles before exhaustion and common sense stopped us. Even a hippopotamus could not have done better. Since it was impossible to rest or sleep on the ground, which was covered by two feet of flood water, we now had to build a hut. Our predicament was so absurd that I remember laughing hysterically before I cried.

In the diary Maisie records that we 'put up a shack and spent the night there' — a bland statement that conceals our prodigious will to survive. I remember helping to build the hut, up to my thighs in water, as the light faded.

Father slashed determinedly at the jungle with my kukri, cutting down bamboo poles, Y-shaped branches and sections of leafy boughs. This was a fairly straightforward task since we were surrounded by a dense forest of tropical scaffolding. Meanwhile, the support staff of architects, engineers, labourers and craftsmen, namely Mum, Maisie, Georgie and me, sorted Father's building materials into a functional structure. Within a few minutes the stout Y-sections were hammered into the soft earth and a row of horizontal bamboo poles were laid over the two long end runners. We had a floor. Next the four longer Y-sections were hammered in at the corners and the same technique used to lay a canopy of thinner bamboo poles. The leafy boughs were piled on top of this to form a reasonably waterproof covering. And we had our roof. Finally, the remaining boughs and poles were stacked against three ends and we had our walls. Then, with a proud sense of achievement, we occupied our new home. Our neighbours on this estate were the Gurkhas of course, with a rustic residence of similar charm.

That night we slept soundly in our own hut in a warm glow of self-satisfaction. We had been faced with a severe challenge but we had won through: it felt immensely reassuring. Sadly we lived in our hut for only a few hours because at first light we were on the move again. However I like to think that it gave rest and protection at a critical stage to other families stumbling through the flooded jungle behind us.

Within a few hours we were free of the flooded valley and ascending the hills which lay across our path to the Hukawng Valley. Five miles further on we reached a stream in full spate, but managed to hop safely across on the large boulders which protruded from the rushing waters. On the far side we stopped for a short rest while the Gurkha *chef de cuisine* created an audacious lunch of plain boiled rice and a spoonful of slippery green things. I had learnt that it was not advisable to enquire too closely what the Gurkhas had collected from the forest – and slippery green things were top of the list. So I munched them and thought of happier times.

After lunch, the path we were following grew progressively steeper. I cast anxious glances at the heavily-laden bull behind me in case it, too, decided to do a kamikaze flip over the edge – but it plodded upwards without protest. At least this ascending path was not knee-deep in water but it was a very tough slog, and I was glad when we called a halt at eight o'clock that night after trekking another five miles. A total of ten miles uphill was a fair day's work in our frail condition. We flopped on the ground beside the track and rolled into our family huddle for warmth. I was asleep within seconds.

Over the next three days we trekked another twenty-seven miles, sleeping on the wet earth each night when exhaustion or darkness stopped us. Our companions during the hours of darkness were leeches, sand-flies and mosquitoes who treated our exposed bodies like a medieval banquet, each guest feasting delicately on their chosen portion. Sand-flies loved eyelids, ears and the backs of hands. Mosquitoes found arms and legs irresistible, while leeches went for the parts which could be politely described as the 'soft bits'. We had all long ago given up trying to deny them.

As usual our progress was across the grain of the Kumon range which entailed trailing up a ridge, descending into a valley, crossing a stream, then up again and down again – and again, and again. Maisie's diary records that on the second day we started at nine in the morning and did not stop until ten that night, having covered twelve miles. Maisie also records that the 'journey climbing high mountains was very tedious'. It was certainly cold that night and for the first time I really missed my bunny rabbit hot-water bottle. On the crest where we lay, the familiar clumps of lantana and rhododendron bushes grew in a more open forest interspersed with birch trees. But it was not until first light that we realised what we had achieved, for we had reached the 4,000-foot-high pass. Many ridges still lay between us and the Hukawng Valley, but it was comforting to know that we were half-way across the barrier of the Kumon range and still full of fight.

It was at this time, somewhere on the way to the Hukawng, that a bizarre and tragic event took place. Much of what happened still remains a mystery to me but it was to cast a long shadow on the psyche of our family. It happened on a day of continuous monsoon storms. I remember the huge physical effort required to climb up a ridge along a track that had been turned into a tumbling brown waterfall. We made walking-sticks out of short bamboo poles and thrust them into the soft earth to steady ourselves. Sometimes we would gain a yard, then lose it in an instant, slithering down before the bamboo pole could hold us. It was wild, brutal stuff – and we fought like animals to get to the top.

However, for some refugees it was too much. They huddled under the trees, peering at us with dull, expressionless eyes that clearly signalled acceptance of their fate: they would not see India after all. Those lying down were already dead. It was only a matter of time before their comrades keeled over and followed them. We stared back at them, knowing that we were powerless to help yet conscious that perhaps next week, or next month, we could be lying by the wayside while others passed us by.

A few yards further on we saw a couple of girls resting beside the track. They were about 15 years old, pale-skinned and with delicate Anglo-Burmese features. It was strange to see youngsters trekking on their own, but even more incongruous were their white school uniforms. Puzzled, we walked on, but we had not gone very far when we came across more teenage girls. They were all dressed in identical white school uniforms.

My parents spoke to them but I have no clear recollection of what was said, except a vague and probably unreliable memory of the words 'Loretto Convent'. Rounding the next spur we saw a large group of about thirty girls climbing the slope: like the ones we had passed they were all dressed in thin white cotton uniforms. They had no protection from the weather, no shoes, and as far as I could make out, no food or baggage. I see them now, as if in a dream, those delicate white butterflies, fluttering along the slope above us.

Nothing prepared us for the shock when we looked again. In the distance a man was helping them across a

particularly bad stretch of track. He looked vaguely familiar – the hair, the outline of the face, the body. It couldn't
be … was it Willie … my eldest brother Willie?

All of a sudden, five voices rang out as one: 'WILLIE!
WILLIE!'

For a few seconds the man looked down. Then he waved
his arms and we heard him reply: 'Father! Mum!'

From this point onwards my mind seems to have been
paralysed by the stunning coincidence which had led us and
my eldest brother to the same spot, at the same time, in the
wilds of the Kumon range, a hundred miles from nowhere,
in the middle of a war. Willie had been living in Rangoon
and, like Richard, had joined the Burma army in 1941.
When the city was about to fall he had sent his wife Della
and their two girls to Lindfield with instructions to wait for
him there, which was why they had refused to leave with
us when we abandoned our home in April. But here he
was, hundreds of miles off course, heading for the
Hukawng. Meanwhile our home, with Della and her
family, was in Japanese hands.

I know that Willie joined us on the trek and that he was
of enormous help, for I clearly remember this strong man
lifting George up the track. Then suddenly he vanished.
No-one ever gave me an explanation. To this day I have no
idea what happened. Was he with us for a day – or longer?
What was he doing there? Where did he go? I never saw
my brother Willie again and I understood he was posted
'Missing. Believed killed.'

An interesting twist to the tale came some years later
when I came across an account which mentioned that the
orphans from the Bishop Strachan Home for Girls were

evacuated to Upper Burma. Several were killed in Japanese air-raids. Eventually about sixty of them arrived in the Sumprabum area, over one hundred miles north of Myitkyina, following the same route we had taken. There the group split up. While thirty-six of the older girls headed for the Hukawng Valley, twenty-five of the younger orphans were taken further northwards into the wild triangle of mountains, where they were discovered by the Japanese.

The route the older girls took through the Kumon range was the same as ours. They travelled for a fortnight through blinding tropical rain, just as we had done, clad only in their thin frocks. Each day they eked out an existence on a cup of tea for breakfast and a plate of rice at the end of a long day's march. An officer, who was escorting the party, decided to go on ahead to secure supplies, and near Maingkwan, sixty-four miles into the Hukawng Valley, he met Clive North, an official in the Burma Frontier Service. North sent him back with provisions for the girls but the officer was unable to reach them, despite several attempts. He later died in the refugee camp at Shingbwiyang.

Meanwhile the older girls, still following the same track we had taken, entered the Hukawng Valley. By the end of the month they had reached Yawbang on the banks of the Tarung River. Though news of this reached North at Shingbwiyang, only twenty-five miles away, he was fully occupied trying to organise food and accommodation for thousands of refugees and Chinese soldiers in the surrounding area. By the time he managed to send help it was too late.

At Yawbang a non-commissioned officer and the two civilian officials in charge of the orphans died. Exhausted, starving and sick, the girls also began to die one by one. Months later when the rains ceased, only seven were still alive and although these reached Shingbwiyang only one eventually reached India.

These, surely, were the girls we saw on the ridges of the Kumon in their white school uniforms, and one of the soldiers with them was Willie. By the time they arrived at Yawbang, we had already reached Shingbwiyang and only two dozen miles separated Willie from us, but it might as well have been a hundred, so atrocious was the weather and the track between us.

By a freakish coincidence Clive North, the Burma Frontier Service official, knew my father and our family. Indeed he had dined with us at Lindfield. Clearly our paths were too entwined for my parents not to have learned what really happened. But no-one ever referred to this incident again. I had to make the discovery for myself.


We rose with the sun and continued our trek through the high mountains. I realise now that, though I was only a child, the perils of the trek had, by degrees, become routine for me. The sharp daily contrasts of life and death, sorrow and laughter, beauty and decay, had become my way of life, for like most children I adapted unconsciously to the new circumstances forced upon me. By contrast, for my parents and Maisie, the past month-and-a-half had been only an episode in their civilised and ordered lives. Their whole experience of this war was tempered by their adult insights and knowledge of the world. Could the trek have changed them as dramatically as it had changed me?

Perhaps not. For unlike Maisie, my awareness was not focused on the journey itself, but on such thrilling moments as when I heard the evocative call of a solitary gibbon. He was perched in the trees of an adjoining ridge not far from two flame-of-the-forest trees which were ablaze with red blossoms. They looked like irides-cent coral reefs in a calm sea, separated from us by a deep valley flecked with wisps of early morning mist. The sun was breaking through the gaps in the clouds, its light and warmth touching the tree-tops where the gibbon lived. In the crystal stillness of the dawn, his voice echoed clear and vibrant across the amphitheatre of the Kumon range: 'Ooooooh Aaah! ... Ooooooh Aaah! .... Ooooooh Aaah! ...'

Fanciful as it may seem, I believe the gibbon was greet-ing the rising sun for the joy of a new day, and I felt a strange empathy with him. We shared the morning, the sun and the life around us; we also shared the rain, the mud and the danger from predators. It was all of a piece. Even his song seemed to hold a sense of reverence and loneliness.

On 29 May 1942 we resumed our trek at seven-thirty in the morning, striding along the track which had a remarkably peaceful look after the nightmare of the past few days. We reached the crest of a ridge after a few miles and innocently looked out across the countryside. There was nothing but an endless green plain. It took about two seconds for the realisation to explode in our numb minds that we had come to the end of the Kumon range. In thir-

teen days we had trekked through sixty-eight miles of
some of the most formidable terrain in Burma – and survived.


A few minutes later we came to a stream about half-way
down the ridge where we relaxed, washed and ate our
lunch. We could see more clearly what lay before us now,
and it was not reassuring. What appeared as a pleasant
stretch of grassland from the top of the ridge was in fact a
limitless plain of brooding primeval jungle. Ahead and to
the left and right, as far as the eye could see to the faint line
of the horizon, was a vast cauldron of steaming vegetation.

The euphoria of the last hour vanished. The adults stood
motionless and subdued as the reality of what they were
seeing sank in. This was the Hukawng Valley, the Valley of
Death where 150 people of the plains had been slaughtered
by Naga headhunters in a ferocious raid only the year
before.

Too young to appreciate the gravity of our situation, I
squeezed myself between my mother and father and held
their hands. When I asked my father where India was, he
pointed across the valley.

'Over there,' he said. 'Only about 250 miles away. Can
you walk that far?'

'Sure I can,' I said. But I had no idea what he meant.

I remember the strange look he gave me as Mum bent
down, holding me so tightly that I could hardly breathe.
But I wriggled out of her arms in my eagerness to see the
Hukawng. I knew that I should pause to offer up my thanks
to the spirits for our deliverance from the mountains. I

should touch the wild flowers, inhale the wind, close my eyes and hold my palms together in contemplation, if only for a second – but George was hobbling briskly downhill, and I could not allow him to be first. I had to win.

The initial descent through open woodland was quite pleasant but the jungle began to close in rapidly as we reached the base of the hill, producing a sweltering atmosphere that sapped our dwindling energy. Moving as cautiously as hunted deer, we stepped into the Valley of Death where the only illumination on the forest floor came from shafts of light which pierced the canopy of branches sixty feet above us. We followed a narrow track through the undergrowth, squelching through ankle-deep mud and pursued by clouds of mosquitoes which spiralled around us. After two miles we saw a deserted Kachin village just off the track which bore the characteristic signs of a trekkers' refuge. Rotting bodies lay in the huts, scattered in the adjoining jungle and even on the path. We hurried past, hardly daring to breathe because the air was so foul. About a mile further on we came across an isolated hut which was free from corpses – something so rare that we hesitated before claiming it for ourselves.

It had been a reasonably easy trek of seven miles, but there was no rejoicing as we settled down for our first night in the Hukawng Valley, plagued by insects which crept out of the decaying bamboo walls. The adults' anxiety puzzled me in view of our remarkable achievement in crossing the Kumon range without serious mishap. My child's ignorance shielded me from what they knew only too well – that we would be lucky to get out of this valley alive.

# 10  *In the Valley of Death*

The euphoria of this first day in the Hukawng was catching. Even the Gurkhas' bull, with a miserly little bag of rice on its back, relished the luxury of a level track as it romped placidly behind us without the slightest need of supervision. We, too, galloped along and surprised ourselves by covering twelve miles before nightfall stopped us at the headwaters of the fast-flowing Tanai river.

The diary records that the track was slushy – again! Evidently there would be no escape from the intractable mud. Churned up by the monsoon rains it lay around us like an ocean, a backdrop to everything we did. When anyone fell now it was not from a slip on a glassy mountain but from sickness and exhaustion. We began to notice an increasing number of dead bodies littering the track. Indeed, death was so common now that it had become a boring event, briefly mourned by a near relative, but generally ignored by the passing crowd. Some days we saw more dead bodies than live trekkers.

My father was not slow to explain the reasons. He did so quite coldly one day, along these lines: 'Our bodies have been weakened by malnutrition so you could die from almost anything, even a cut finger. We have no medicines except a little quinine. Do not eat or drink anything except cooked food and boiled water. And let me know the moment you are ill. Is that clear?'

'Yes, Dr Brookes! Thank you, Dr Brookes!' I whispered obsequiously.

But he was right to remind us that dangerous germs and moulds thrive in the humid jungle, some capable of transforming a leech bite into an open wound several inches wide. We had already seen people staggering along the trail with maggots burrowing into these Naga sores, as they were called – a sight so awful that the memory still disturbs me.

Of course it was the monsoon that was ultimately responsible for these deaths. At any other time the track and the jungle would have been dry and the streams would have been placid trickles rather than raging torrents. Crossing the Hukawng and the mountain ranges would have been relatively quick and painless; now it seemed only a matter of time before the germs that killed the others killed us.

This, then, was our introduction to the Valley of Death. My father's message was clear enough, but hunger is an insatiable demon. Night and day it filled my imagination with curries and cream cakes while I chewed and swallowed fresh air.

When we stopped for a break next day, I noticed a huge tree with reddish fruit that looked like mangoes. My resistance collapsed instantly and Father's commands went clean out of my head. I had a single overpowering vision: FOOD!

Moving warily, I crept in a wide arc towards the tree while my family rested in a small clearing. I still remember the feeling of breathless elation when I saw the windfalls at the base of the tree. But they were not mangoes.

'To hell with mangoes,' I thought, 'I'll eat them anyway.'

When I sank my teeth into one it was juicy but intensely sour. But hungry little boys are not choosy, so I ate it all. And another. I was just about to start on a third when a stern voice rang through the jungle.

'Stephen! Stephen! Where are you.'

Fear of discovery plunged me instantly into near hysteria. I dropped the guilty fruit in fright, wiped my mouth to erase the evidence, then shouted in a submissive, baby voice, 'Coming Father' and dived back through the undergrowth. Alas, the undergrowth was a massive thicket of what, I now believe, were giant nettles. They towered above me, but since I had never seen such plants before I did not realise that the inch-long needles had a sting like a hornet's. My threadbare clothes gave me no protection.

Suddenly my whole body caught fire as my jangling nerves registered 'POISON' and went into overdrive. I remember the pain – such excruciating pain. In my ignorance I assumed malign jungle spirits were attacking me for raiding the fruit tree. Jeeeesusss! Was I scared! I imagined invisible evil nats closing in, tearing at me with their claws, sinking their teeth into my arms. Perhaps even killing me?

'Run Brookesie,' I screamed. 'Run.'

I stumbled and crashed through more nettles on the way out, and by the time I reached my family I was in a dreadful state. Awash with poison, I swooned, shivered, cried, turned into a lumpy pineapple – and damn near died. I am sure Father must have known what these plants were, yet I cannot remember being treated with anything.

When I was able to speak out of my swollen face I told my family that I had simply gone into the jungle for a quiet pee and got lost. Then, when Father called, I had run back through the bushes, and been bitten by these things. No one disputed my story. I never referred to the episode again, though a day after eating those unknown fruit I was struck by the mother of all constipations.

That night we slept in a deserted Kachin hut. I remember it well for one reason – it was dry. The joy of sleeping off the ground on something dry was overpowering. By popular demand it was decided to spend another day there. The Gurkhas marked the occasion by cooking some mashed vegetables and spices for dinner. It was a simple meal but Maisie notes that we 'had a good feed'. My portion, heavily scented with wood smoke, tasted unbelievably delicious.

During the course of the next seven days we trekked fifty-two miles, most of it along the valley through which the Tanai flowed. It was hot, humid and thoroughly unpleasant. Clouds of midges followed us, flying into our hair, ears and noses, tormenting us with their high-pitched whine and fiery stings. There was no respite either when we waded through the flooded areas, where shoals of voracious six-inch tiger leeches latched on to our bodies to drink our blood. Since we had no means of preventing any of these attacks, we just put up with them, trekking on silently in regimental formation.

It was about this time that I once again lost control of my craving for food. Clearly my first experience of eating forbidden fruit should have been 'character-forming', as Willie used to say, but the devil of hunger will go to any limit. Besides, as I had not been found out the first time there was an excellent chance of getting away with it again.

And so one day, during a rest period, like a thief at night I sneaked away to a bush of taparies (physallis) which I had spied growing in an abandoned patch of slash-and-burn forest. The urge to fill my belly was overpowering. Heedless of the consequences I plucked handfuls of fruit, ripped open the 'Chinese lanterns' and collected the berries inside. Tense with excitement I hid behind a tree and started to eat them. But I had made two cardinal errors: they were green, unripe fruit, and I had left a trail of husks in my wake that any fool could follow.

My teeth worked through the unripe fruit like a frantic harvester shovelling corn. I hardly paused for breath. My cheeks were stuffed but still I chewed, savouring the pleasure of crunching something solid. I swallowed the raw pulp in impatient gulps. What bliss it was as I patted the devil in my belly and sighed contentedly.

Gorged and happy, I looked up from the log where I was sitting. My father was standing silently before me. How short are the pleasures of illicit conduct. Time and again through life I was to learn that stolen fruit of any sort are forever tainted. Nothing can be 'unstolen', any more than a hateful word can be unsaid – except perhaps by love and forgiveness.

Father's face was stern: there was no love in his eyes.

'Have you eaten these, Stephen?' he asked, flinging a fistful of crushed 'Chinese lanterns' at my feet. His voice was harsh, dangerous.

I could not speak. Eyes on the ground, I nodded.

'You knew they were green. Unripe?'

I nodded again. What I wanted to say was: 'Father I'm sorry. For Christ's sake forgive me.' But I remained silent.

'You know green fruit will give you diarrhoea.'

'Father ... er ... please Father ... yes I know.'

'Yet you deliberately ate them. You knew the consequences, yet you ate them.'

'Father ... er ...'

'Speak up. You knew the consequences and yet you ate these green fruit?'

'Yes ... Father ... I'm ... I was hungry.'

'Well, you know the rules of the trek. If any of us falls ill and cannot walk, that person will be left behind, because we cannot risk the lives of the others for the sake of one person. Do you understand that?'

I was in turmoil. But Father rapped out again: 'Do you understand that?'

'Yes Father ... can I go now and see Mum?'

'Then let me make this clear. When you get diarrhoea, as you surely will ... I shall leave you behind. Do you hear me? ... I shall leave you behind. I will not risk the lives of the others for your sake. Is that clear?'

I was stunned. But then again, I knew Father was right. Why should Mum and Maisie and Georgie stay here and die because of my frailty.

'I said: is that clear?'

I looked up at my father's face. It was the face of the Angel of Death. I thought I was going to faint, but I struggled to say, 'Yes ... it's clear ... thank you, Father.'

He turned on his heel without another word and I watched his back as he walked away. He had condemned me to death and left me alone, on a log, in the middle of the Valley of Death. I wanted to cry but could not. What a senseless life this was: to die from eating nothing or to die from eating something – what difference did it make?

I was a child, yet on this trek I had also become a man, wise beyond my years, for circumstances had made me so. Gradually in my dull head, thudding with confusion and misery, a tiny flame flickered: 'I will not die,' said the man/child. 'I WILL NOT DIE. I WILL . . . NOT . . . DIE.'

Yet I wished I had said 'sorry' to Father. I had done wrong and I should have apologised. Maybe later, I thought. But in real life you seldom get a second chance – and that's the tragedy of it.

In spite of my uncertain future in the realm of the living, something my father taught me as a boy at Lindfield echoed in my head: 'Remember this, my son: do not let the sun go down on your wrath.'

I had not forgotten his injunction. Far from it. But I was as stubborn and strong-willed as my father. We were two of a kind, and in the cauldron of the Hukawng a future Major Brookes was being created.

'On your feet Brookesie,' I said to myself. 'Steady the Buffs! Steady there, that man. Face your front.'

I had to remain seated for a while as I did not trust my legs to carry me. At last, still feeling slightly queasy, I stepped out of the forest and joined my family as they got ready to leave. I was so fond of wandering off into the jungle on my own that Mum had hardly missed me.

'Hi! Stevie,' said George. 'Are you OK?'

'Yep! Fine Georgie,' I replied. I punched the air with my fist and yelled 'Tarzan!'

'Me Jane,' lisped my brother, executing a neat shimmy in the slush.

We burst into spontaneous laughter as only children can. Then I walked solemnly to my position as the regimental rearguard and the Great Trek continued. 'Sorry, Father' I said in my head, but it was pointless – and I knew it.

I did indeed have violent diarrhoea, but at the first sign I slipped into the jungle so that no one would see me. For a few days I suffered in silence and there were moments when I thought the game was up as my strength steadily drained away. But I was so bloody-minded in my determination to survive that in the end the germs left me for easier prey. My strong constitution defeated them, and for that I have to thank my mother and my father.

About this time, what seemed to me a trifling event took place. That it was blown up into something worthy of a court martial, or even the death penalty was, I believe, entirely due to Father's and Maisie's frayed nerves.

We had stopped for the night in a deserted Kachin village after a particularly slow and exhausting trek of fifteen miles. Rotting bodies lay in most of the huts, giving off such a foul stench that we gladly made our way out of the village and bedded down on the earth.

The inky black night was filled with the usual assortment of biting insects, but we were too tired to notice. We lay in a long row under our damp blanket like a plate of grilled sardines: Father on the left, then Mum, George and me, with Maisie on my right. Sleep came instantly.

At some point during the night, this tranquil family scene was shattered by a deafening scream about an inch from my right ear. I shot bolt upright, crazed with fright, staring wide-eyed into the darkness and letting out a blood-curdling scream which was answered by another blast in my right ear from Maisie. It was enough to put a wandering tiger off human meat for the rest of its life. I saw a black shape scurrying away from Maisie. Before I could let rip again the authoritative voice of the Major rang out.

'Shut up! SHUT UP IMMEDIATELY. Stephen and Maisie – do you hear me? Stop this screaming immediately.

I was just beginning to enjoy myself, though I had absolutely no idea what Maisie was screaming about.

'Why are you screaming, Stephen?' demanded Father.

I had no real answer, so I implicated my sister: 'Oh ... er ... Maisie ... Father.'

'Maisie,' roared the impatient voice, 'why were you screaming?'

By this time Maisie had started to cry as well. Then she uttered the fateful words: 'The Gurkha had his hand under the blanket, Daddy. He was touching me.'

Great balls of fire! I thought Maisie had been attacked by something interesting, like a tiger. But a Gurkha? How boring.

'Quick. Under the blanket. Close your eyes. There's going to be Gurkha blood on the ground,' I said to George.

Father's growl in the pitch blackness was answered by Mum's anxious voice: 'Willie. Willie. Be calm. Willie, don't lose your temper.'

There was a quivering wail from the darkness on the right: 'Sahib. Sahib. Sorry, Sahib. Sorry, missie. Very sorry, Sahib.'

Of course no one had such a thing as a torch, but Father fanned the embers and very soon we had some light on the subject – namely, the Gurkha. Every one was fully awake by this time. Father was looking for his pistol to shoot the man who'd dared to touch his daughter. But Mum had hidden it. They argued. Meanwhile the Gurkha's wife joined in. She bawled at her husband and cuffed him. Maisie, the focus of all this attention, sniffed loudly. She was obviously enjoying this diversion. For the two youngest, however, this was adult burlesque at its most outrageous. George and I immediately lost interest. We lay down and went back to sleep. I could not imagine what the fuss was about. By all means have a rumpus if someone was stealing food or being eaten by a wild beast. But 'touching', whatever that was – how boring.

At the next village, which was Maingkwan, Father dismissed the Gurkhas and paid them off. And so we parted from these amiable companions who had shared the terrors of the Great Trek with us for almost a month. Together we had struggled for 132 miles across the Kumon range and part of the Hukawng Valley, forging a relationship of mutual trust and admiration.

Gurkhas have a great sense of humour and I was going to miss them. They never failed to respond with a rousing, *'Shabash Sahib! Shabash!'* (Well done Sir! Well done!) when I greeted them with the war cry: *'Aiyo Gurkhali'* and flourished my silver-handled kukri at imaginary *dushman* (enemies). But Father could never forgive a man who crept about in the dark touching up his daughter.

Maingkwan was a village with a semblance of civilisation we had not seen since leaving Myitkyina over a month ago. A track broad enough for carts and motor-vehicles connected it to Mogaung on the main railway line over one hundred miles to the south. The evacuees who chose this track into the Hukawng Valley avoided the winding footpath over the Kumon range which we had taken. I suppose you could call them timid – even intelligent – for following an easier route lined with food dumps.

News that the Japanese had not only taken Mogaung but had advanced some distance up this broad track fuelled wild rumours of their imminent arrival at Maingkwan. What an ignoble end it would be for us and the other weary trekkers from the Kumon range if we had dodged the enemy at Myitkyina and taken a 235-mile Cook's 'Tour of Hell', only to find them waiting patiently for us at the roadside.

So on 9 June, without the Gurkhas, my family set out again at a steady pace. Over two days we trekked eighteen miles along a difficult track deep in mud with occasional patches of sinking sand. This was the area where the floodwaters, swamps and tributary rivers in the Hukawng Valley joined to form the Chindwin river. From here an immense volume of water flowed southwards for 500 miles to its confluence with the Irrawaddy in the plains near Mandalay.

At this time of year these rivers were about 150 yards wide at this point, with a vicious current that swirled past alarmingly. The only means of crossing them was a raft made from logs and bamboo poles roped together. My abiding memory is of two dozen refugees, most of them non-swimmers like myself, balancing on this crazy device just inches above the water, while the Kachins strained to haul it against the force of the current to the other bank. I do not think I could have handled more than one crossing of each river without a severe panic attack.

An official government report written soon after these events states that during this period 2,000 refugees were crossing these rivers by ferry each day. This crossing-place was a nightmare as thousands of refugees including deserters, Chinese army thugs, the dead and the dying, crammed the banks on either side.

Once we were over the Tanai river we trekked for six miles to a Kachin village near another river, the Tarung. Here, once again, hundreds of refugees were forced to halt. Like us they poured in from the Tanai river crossing but were unable to cross the Tarung since the operation here was much slower.

As more and more refugees piled up along the riverbank, fighting for a place on the tiny rafts, the situation deteriorated into anarchy. Military deserters with weapons seized the rafts and boats to get their own men across, shooting anyone who resisted them. Looters and thugs preyed on the weak. No matter where I looked there was a human being in torment, pleading, arguing or dying.

We waited here for three awful days while Father tried to make arrangements for a crossing, a critical matter by the third day when both George and Maisie became ill. It was now or never. Perhaps Father's uniform helped or money

changed hands or his decision to carry his pistol promi-
nently had some effect. Whatever it was, we finally crossed
the Tarung on 15 June and sought shelter in a Kachin
village.

Without a doubt, we and every one of the thousands
who were ferried across the Tarung and the Tanai rivers in
1942 owe a debt of gratitude to the Kachins and the Nagas.
These simple jungle people risked their lives day after day
to help us to safety, even though their own hold on life in
this harsh valley was tenuous at best. In return the armies
and civilians polluted their rivers, destroyed their homes
and infected their people with diseases. What is more, as
with many of the ordinary people sucked into this war,
their heroism and self-sacrifice went unsung. Meanwhile,
those responsible for the débâcle in Burma sipped their
sherries in the comfort of Simla, Delhi and London. After
all, Burma was a 'sideshow'. There was no glory or
promotion there.

I pay my tribute now to the Kachins and Nagas of the
Hukawng Valley for their heroic help to the refugees in
1942. '*Chay-zu-tin-de.*' Thank you, brothers. May the spirits
of your ancestors never leave the fireside of your homes.


As June passed the monsoon seemed to be growing more
severe. The influx of refugees from the Mogaung/
Maingkwan route only intensified the appalling suffering.
Cholera and malaria raged unchecked. The dead lay piled
beside the track, while those about to die tottered past,
helpless and weeping. As for the Chinese soldiers, their
dead lay everywhere. It was here at Yawbang near the

Tarung river that my brother Willie and the girls of the orphanage were to meet their end. But I knew nothing of this as we splashed past on the next leg of our journey.

After the second crossing we had hardly walked a couple of miles when a storm sent us scurrying deeper into the jungle for shelter. Huddling under a tree we saw the ideal refuge: a *nat-za-yat* or spirit house, in a small glade partly obscured by dense jungle. Built on a platform which rested on four wooden stilts about ten feet tall, it looked just like a child's deserted tree-house. There was ample space underneath it for the five of us to shelter comfortably.

The spirit house itself was a small bamboo hut with an elegant thatch roof that curled upwards at the four corners like a jester's hat. Entry was via a log with footholds cut into it. The hut itself and the surrounding area were festooned with bamboo poles from which hung faded pennants and folded palm leaves, giving the place an air of jubilation and watchful calm. There was some speculation about the nature of the inner sanctum, but Mum was reluctant to provoke the spirits by careless conversation. She told us to keep quiet, behave ourselves and be respectful.

In spite of this warning I was boiling with curiosity. Were there jewels, idols, gold? One glance into the home of the spirits would satisfy me. There would never be another chance like this. But the others were only interested in moving on. They stared morosely at the rain and set out briskly down the track the moment it slackened. It was too much for me. Looking as innocent as I could, I slipped into the jungle, calling to Mum that I had to go to the toilet and would catch up with her shortly. In a few seconds I was back at the spirit house and clambering up the log.

The room was about six feet square, split into two sections by a plaited bamboo screen about a foot high. The floor of the section nearest the door was covered by a soft bamboo mat on which I presume people sat and prayed. The section beyond the screen was clearly the inner sanctum where fires and candles had been lit regularly. The woven bamboo wall was stained dark brown from the smoke of many fires, and feathers and ash lay in the hearth. From the walls and the ceiling hung strips of coloured cloth, and shapes made from folded ferns and palm fronds.

My eyes were instantly drawn to a square of coloured cloth in the centre of the inner sanctum – for on it were coins. Silver coins and copper coins, lots of them spread out before me, glittering like a pirate's hoard. I was stunned. Acting on a foolish impulse, I scooped up a few, thrusting them into my pocket before clambering down the steps. A few minutes later I rejoined my family.

A couple of miles further on we stopped for a rest. But I was careless, or guilty, for without my being aware of it, two coins fell out of my torn pocket as I sat down on the grass.

After a few minutes I heard my father say: 'Is that yours Stephen?' He pointed at the grass beside me.

I glanced down and – I wished I was dead. Mum shook her head in despair: there was no point in denying it.

'Yes, Father,' I replied.

'Where did you get them from?'

'I took them from that spirit house.' What a relief to be honest.

'You stole them from the Kachin nat house?' He looked at me with those hard eyes again. Mum was getting agitated.

'Yes, Father. I'm sorry. Sorry, Mum.'

He stared at me, weighing up my punishment. Mum looked as if she was about to get up and beat me. I looked down, waiting.

'That was wrong, Stephen. You know that don't you?'

'Yes, Father. I was wrong. I'm really sorry. I'll never do that again.' He let out a deep sigh of frustration.

'Go back,' he said, 'and return every coin to the nat house.'

My nerves tingled with fright and I felt worse when I looked back down the jungle trail. Were those people lying in the jungle really dead or were they waiting to grab my legs as I passed? I was also terrified of climbing back into the spirit house knowing that I had desecrated the spirits' home. But the punishment was right and I knew it.

'We will go on, so you had better hurry if you want to catch up with us,' said my father, without the slightest concern.

I stood up as they prepared to leave. Only Georgie waved as I picked up the coins and walked back down the track. Within a couples of minutes I had lost sight of my family. I was on my own.

The only thought in my head was: 'Steady the Buffs! Steady!' It was two miles to the hut and two miles back. Then I had to find the others, who would have gone on for a another couple of miles. Crikey! Six miles in the jungle on my own. Yet I knew I could do it, because I had wandered in the jungles of Maymyo with my Daisy air rifle since I was nine years old. Anyway, it was my fault and I had a chance to put things right and redeem myself. It had to be done. The only real worry was the reaction of the spirits in the *nat-za-yat*.

Summoning my courage I quickened my pace, jogging along where the ground was reasonably firm or moving straight into the jungle to cut out the bends on the track. I kept as far away as I could from the dead people lying in the jungle. When I finally reached the hut I stood very still for a while with my palms together in supplication. Then I climbed the log stairs.

I experienced a dramatic sensation of warmth. You might think it had something to do with my exertions. But you would be wrong. It was a strange, welcoming warmth, a distinctive presence. I felt I had been forgiven by the spirits. It was a boy's prank that had gone wrong and I had returned to say sorry. I felt their absolution and a real sense of peace.

I respectfully returned the coins to their rightful home. Then I held my palms together and asked for forgiveness.

The sun was going down as I ran like a young fawn through the jungle. I felt elated that my mistake had been put right. My kukri was tied round my waist but I did not draw it. Somehow I knew I was safe; I knew nothing sinister would happen to me because the spirits would let me pass. It seemed I had run for a very long time before I glimpsed the figures of my family. Then I was home, with Mum holding me close while Father patted my back.

'Well done. Well done, son,' was all he said. But there was pride in his voice and it was all I wanted to hear. Nothing mattered any more as I strode with my family, delighting in Mum's soft, warm hands, Maisie's smile and Georgie's broad grin. I was forgiven.

As night drew in it began to rain heavily. Wearily we looked for shelter. I sensed that by now we were beginning to struggle to cover a moderate distance without a rest. As our strength waned, so the difficulties imposed by the monsoon increased. We had thrown an insolent challenge to the Valley of Death by entering its untamed kingdom during the height of the rainy season. Now, clearly, each one of us was to be severely tested.

# 11  *Through the Chinese Ambush*

It was 16 June 1942 and we had been on the run from the Japanese army for exactly two months. We were still ahead – but only just. Though the monsoon had reduced the speed of both sides to an agonising crawl, we had no doubt that the Japanese would make a determined foray up this track as soon as the rains stopped. Being less than keen to make their acquaintance, we would have to increase our pace over the next stage if we were to get out of their way. But it was noticeable that my brother and sister were beginning to falter. Lion-hearted Georgie looked like a walking skeleton and Maisie seemed to be in the grip of a mysterious fever. Lying in the dark that night, unable to influence the outcome in any way, I felt the first tremor of doubt that this trek would have a happy ending.

The unusual bright sunshine next morning soothed my jaded nerves. How reassuring it was to wake up in this jungle, a thousand miles from home, and hear Mum and

154

Maisie gossiping in a dilapidated bamboo hut as though they were in the kitchen at Lindfield. Then to hear Georgie talking to himself, as he swatted the insects that had invaded his body during the night. His speciality was hunting body lice – those nasty little creatures that hid in the folds of our clothes until nightfall, then swarmed out to munch our skin while we slept. And there was my dear defiant father, the Major. I giggled as I watched him march purposefully through the undergrowth near the hut in his bare feet and ragged uniform: shoulders back, head high, muttering prayers to his God. Occasionally he would stop, grind his teeth and groan in frustration. I guessed he was arguing with his Maker for dumping him and his family in this lethal greenhouse – an unjust reward for a lifetime of devotion. As I watched him, a thought seeded itself in my mind which eventually broke my childhood faith. Up to then I had always believed that things actually happened when you prayed. Now I guessed that in reality there was no trade-off, no quid pro quo, with my father's Christian God. A vague notion that complete self-reliance was the only solution in a crisis began to stir in my mind.

After a breakfast of plain tea and cold rice, we set out to face the perils of the day. The shafts of sunlight had transformed the forest into a vast theatre lit by dazzling spotlights. They shone through gaps in the high canopy on to tree trunks, flowers and branches, turning them into a wonderland of many colours. I realised for the first time that the leaves were not drab green, but a delicate mixture of greens, yellows and browns. The round pillars of tree-trunks over sixty feet high were gnarled and streaked with creepers and layers of dark green moss. And from the highest branches hung endless loops of vines and trailing plants like fluted velvet curtains edged with lace.

But the sight that enchanted me then, and still delights my mind's eye, were the clusters of elegant orchids on the branches. They glistened in the rays of the spotlights high above me, like phantoms from another world: luxuriant spikes of colour that brought back memories of the orchids hanging in the porch of my lost home. I stood still, transfixed by their beauty. If ever there was a moment when I sensed my mother's 'oneness of life', it was here, in the Valley of Death. I could not explain it, but there seemed to be a connection between the living trees and the lifeless human remains at their roots. The wind on my face blended with the scents of the jungle and of decomposing flesh. The sound of human voices mingled with the rustle of the leaves.

I rushed to catch up with my family, calling to them to share my joy. But they walked on, weighed down by adult thoughts and fears. They had not lifted up their eyes. And even if they had, they had looked but not seen, thinking only of survival. Yet for me, the trek that morning had been an enchantment and I was exhilarated. Here was magic; here was the meeting-place of the nats.

By noon we were worn out, so we stopped in a clearing for a ration of boiled water followed by an exciting lunch comprising:

*Starters*
Sip of Tea (local mouldy leaf)

*Main Course*
One Ball, Stale Boiled Rice
With Boiled Substance (possibly non-poisonous?)

*Pudding*
(Out of stock)

Frankly, the luncheon menu was getting worse as the weeks went by. However I decided it would be unwise to complain to the chef, my mother, in view of the uncertain sense of humour of the management, my father, who was inclined to load his pistol when we stopped in case an edible piece of meat ambled past.

Still ravenous after the meal, I clutched my empty stomach, lay down on the grass and dozed happily for half-an-hour in a world of endless chocolate cake. Beside me, Mum puffed contentedly on one of the revolting cigarettes she made out of Naga tea-leaves and a piece of paper. Gone were the days when I used to help her open the vacuum-packed tin of fifty Gold Flake cigarettes sent out from England. Her Naga tea came in small bamboo tubes, like a plug of shredded tobacco. When we needed a cup of tea we scraped some of the pressed leaves into a larger bamboo tube and poured hot water into it. It was as simple as that and it tasted heavenly. Most things do when you are starving.

When we decided to rejoin the obstacle course, we found we were alone in the jungle. However we were not unduly worried and blithely walked on up the steep narrow track, which was cut into the side of a ridge, ending in a series of sharp bends.

Suddenly we noticed a party of Chinese soldiers coming down the track towards us. All of them were armed. Two soldiers were ahead of the others but we lost sight of them when they passed us and continued round the next bend. Suddenly their voices rang out behind us in unintelligible but very hostile-sounding Chinese – something like: '*Wan-che, yeh-sung quan-li.*'

We had no idea what it meant then, but looking back I am certain it was a signal that said: 'OK. The coast is clear.'

Without warning the remaining Chinese stormed into us, hustling us, pushing us, shouting in their strange language. There must have been a dozen of them. Their rifle-bolts clicked loudly as they slid bullets into firing-chambers. Fingers gripped triggers and barrels were swung round to point at each one of us.

There was pandemonium. My father responded fiercely. There were several men around him. I saw Mum and Maisie clutching one another but I could not see George. Suddenly I was hit in the chest by a soldier wielding a rifle, prompting me to raise my hands smartly above my head. Someone had taken hold of Georgie, who had his hands above his head as well. What the devil was going on? Who were these people? After a second or two the answer flashed into my mind. We were being ambushed by remnants of the Chinese Fifth Army.

We had passed hundreds of these men in the past few weeks. They had been outmanoeuvred and beaten by the Japanese in the battles south of Mandalay. In the collapse and retreat that followed, some had made it back to Yunnan

before the Burma Road was cut near Lashio. The remainder wandered about in the jungles of northern Burma,
some heading for India and the rest trying to reach China
via the Hukawng Valley. Those who were not yet dying
robbed the refugees who were about to die.

Maisie and Mum began to cry out as the pack closed in.

Father lost his temper. 'Don't you dare touch them,' he
bawled at a Chinese officer. The fellow had a loaded pistol
which he shoved against Father's head.

'*Guan-zi! zhu-ban.*'

'I am a Major. This is my family. Put that pistol away.'

'*Shuz!*'

He was going to shoot Father.

'Put that pistol down. I am an officer.'

'*Shuz!*'

Mother screamed 'Willie! Don't lose your temper. Let
them take what they want.'

I thought: 'Please Father, don't reach for your pistol. If
you do, we are all dead.'

The soldiers began pushing the women around, tugging
at their clothes. What should I do? What could I do? Oh
my dear mother.

There was little hope of me doing anything because a
lout shoved his rifle into my face. It was about six inches
from my eyes. I looked straight down the black barrel while
his finger curled round the trigger. I was about to die. Time
missed a beat. The still-picture of that rifle-barrel in my
face and the finger on the trigger has stayed for ever frozen
in my mind.

Mother's bag was ransacked and the contents flung out
on the track. The small amount of food we had was taken.

I remember seeing a golden brooch in a soldier's hand which had probably been wrenched from Mum's secret hiding-place in the bag. Now the ambush had really got out of hand, for I knew they would not be satisfied until they had searched all of us for hidden jewellery.

Maisie had her hands up, her face ashen and her eyes wide and staring. She stood like a statue, waiting for the end, her personal things scattered around her.

Then it was my turn. An evil-looking Chinese, not much taller than me, started bawling again. Didn't they have manners in China? Besides, shouting at me was pointless because I had no idea what he was saying. My hands were still raised and I felt utterly numb. My mouth was dry and I was terrified that this blockhead would slip in the slush as we struggled and accidentally blow my head off.

He ripped my blazer pockets off, rifled though my coloured stones, bits of metal, string, coins, rubies, pen-knife and bullets. He kept what he wanted, then threw my treasure, which I had carried for almost one thousand miles, into the slush. Then he kicked my tin of malted milk powder into the bushes. There was not much left in it but it was our lifeline to survival.

'*Zan-wei!*' he hissed.

What the hell did that mean? Was he angry because I had nothing of real value to steal? The Chinese officer thrust his pistol against Father's neck and began to drag him away, probably with the intention of shooting him.

Mother called out: 'No! No! My husband. No shoot. No shoot. Willie, stay calm, stay calm.'

Georgie was beside me, hands raised, but another Chinese was pushing him with a rifle. When he stumbled on his lame feet I held my breath, because I knew that if he fell Father would start shooting. Georgie was his special responsibility, his cross, and no one harmed Georgie and lived. I wished I could see the orchids before I died, but I dared not even twitch in case this Chinese bandit treated it as an excuse to pull the trigger.

I tried not to look at Maisie and Mum but I could hear Father yelling at a bastard who was trying to get at Maisie's clothing.

I stared back with intense hatred at the fellow who was glowering at me and I made a vow: 'I will remember your face. When I grow up I will kill you, I promise. Unlike you I will not hesitate, you son of a pig. If Mum and Maisie are harmed I want vengeance. No matter how long it takes, no matter what it takes, I will get you in the end. I will never forget. Get behind me God, I suspected all along You were useless in a crisis.'

For the first time in my life I felt a terrible darkness in my soul. Like an explosion of black bile the torrent of anger beat against my temples. This was my family, these were my people and I loved them dearly. Yet these creatures came into our lives and touched us with their evil.

Suddenly from where the track curved behind the forested ridge, a shrill voice rang out: '*Wu-chi. Yang-zo.*'

The two lookouts were calling. It sounded urgent and probably meant: 'Let's go! People coming.'

In a flash the weapons were withdrawn. The soldiers moved rapidly down the track, giving us a passing shove and a swipe as they went. I cursed them silently: 'Get out of my life you Chinese animals, and may you rot in hell before the month is through.'

Finally, it was over. It seemed like an hour but the attack had probably taken no more than fifteen minutes. We had been ambushed and robbed but we were alive. Well, up to a point I was alive, but something serious had happened to me, though I could not understand it or explain it. My face was burning hot and my vision was blurred while my hands were ice-cold and shaking. Not just with shock – but with humiliation and rage.

We ignored the group of people whose unscheduled arrival had ended a scene which nearly became a blood-bath. They gazed blankly at our scattered possessions and passed on without comment; for on this road, it was only a day or a week or an hour that separated the living from the dead. Their looks seemed to say: 'So it's your turn today, my friends. How sad. But our own ordeal awaits us on the morrow.'

Although the Chinese had gone, the atmosphere was still supercharged with tension. We could not look at each other, nor did we speak. I squatted down to pick my coloured stones out of the slush. But in the process I real-ised, rather sadly, that the Chinese thug was right, for what I called my treasures were junk. In another time and place they had sparkled and shone like diamonds in my childish imagination. But the soldier had seen them for what they really were: lifeless stones, just trash. I left them where they died, for I could not make them live again.

I found the tin of malted milk in the bushes and brushed the muck off the sides. Then I took off my torn blazer and flung it into the jungle, first removing my enamelled butterfly badge from the lapel. Apart from that, all I had left now was my Gurkha kukri and the frayed shorts and shirt I wore.

The others were grim-faced as we trudged silently up the narrow track. I kept my eyes averted, only snatching a brief glance at Mum and Maisie as I took my place at the rear of the column. It was easy to see that my father was seething with fury from his stiff posture and clenched fists as he led the family along the path. We had hardly walked half-a-mile before his suppressed anger exploded. He roared like a cornered beast, his arms flailing wildly at the invisible Chinese who tormented him. Thank heaven my mother's words had cooled his head during the ambush. Yet his anger seemed to ignite something in me. I instantly felt the throbbing in my head and the cold sweat on my hands. Damn the Chinese! Would we ever be free of the poison they had left behind?

I stepped quickly into the jungle as I saw him wrench his pistol off his belt. He was not going to do something stupid and hurt someone, was he? Was he going back down the track after the soldiers? Unsure of what to do, we stood absolutely still while he flourished it for a few moments. Finally, with a bitter cry he flexed his arm back and hurled the weapon into the jungle. I can still see the heavy pistol sailing over the bushes in a steep arc before it crashed into the thick wall of jungle and disappeared in a shower of falling leaves. For better or worse, the means of killing in defence of his family was gone from Father's survival kit for ever. From now on, we would have to be as meek as lambs in this forest of wolves – which was going to be difficult, given the Major's temperament. Perhaps it was just as well, because in the recent crisis the pistol had proved to be a provocation rather than a deterrent. Only a year earlier Father had taught the three of us to shoot, using this same pistol and a sardine tin as a target. When I had held it in my hand then, it felt like a cannon and I recalled the sense of power it gave me. Yet today it was like a fair-ground popgun in this violent world.

After a pause my father pulled his haversack off his shoulder, plunged his right hand into the side-pocket and extracted his military medals. Without a second glance he threw them into the jungle, making me wince with sadness as I saw them go. I knew these medals well because I used to dress up in my brother-in-law's army uniform and play with them when we were at Lindfield. I am certain there were five and there may have been more. They were awarded to Father for his service to his king and country. Once the old warrior had worn them with pride but now they were junk. Priceless medals thrown away, just like my treasured stones, because they no longer had power to gladden the heart, or evoke the magic of happier days. I did not realise until several weeks later that Mum had quietly picked up the medals from the jungle and concealed them from my father.

Looking back now, I can understand my father's frustration, humiliation and pent-up anger that day. It had been a terrible year for him. Month after month this proud man's authority and control had been remorselessly chipped away by events. Finally the warrior had been unable to defend his family in the classic confrontation of arms. For a person like my father, such an outcome was utterly demeaning, yet he had no choice. It was a terrible price to pay in spiritual currency.

I understood a little of his agony because I felt it also with a child's intensity. In fact the impact of the Chinese ambush was severe enough to stay with me for most of my life. Yet we never mentioned this incident again.

One strange effect of the ambush was the loss of cohesion of our family group. From this point, our strict regimental formation fragmented into a loose collection of individuals wandering on their own. Sometimes I trotted past the group until I was a quarter of a mile in front, or I would sit in the jungle alone with my thoughts, rejoining the others later when I felt like it. It was during a solitary moment such as this that I committed my greatest transgression in the Hukawng.

I was resting in the jungle, waiting for my family to catch up with me, when curiosity and hunger drove me to consider the exciting possibility of prising open the tin of malted milk-powder. Implausible as it may seem, my original intention was honest, for I only wanted to see if the Chinese soldier had damaged the contents. I had faithfully carried the heavy tin over endless swamps and mountains and never once opened it myself. But when the lid was lifted off it revealed a layer of delicious food that I now found irresistible. There was little time for guilt or reflection as I devoured spoonfuls of the sweet powder. Once I had started it was difficult to stop, but when I did there was not much left.

At our next wayside stop I passed Father the tin as usual to share out our ration. I was foolish enough to believe that after the experience of the Chinese ambush he would be understanding. But his fury was the worst I had ever seen and I was relieved that he had thrown away his pistol. I was spared punishment only because Mum kept on repeating, 'He's only a child, Willie. He's only a child. Don't be angry.' He scraped the tin, ignoring me completely as he offered the others a small helping of milk-powder each before hurling the offending tin and the spoon into the jungle.

I knew very well that we depended on each other for survival. I had honoured this solemn trust for several months. But now, weak-willed and driven by hunger, I had let the side down. I looked at my father's face and in his sad eyes I saw his reproach. I knew there was nothing I could say that would make any difference.

As a penalty I was given the heavy flask of water to carry. It was so large that when I held it by the handle the base just cleared the ground, bumping against my ankle with every step. Worse still, it held several pints and when it was full it was so heavy that it wrenched my shoulders – but I was glad to suffer.

That day we trekked a total of eight miles through the jungle. When the evening shadows began to lengthen we stopped by a stream, lay down on the wet ground and slept the sleep of the dead. It had been a bloody day and I was relieved that it had ended. Maybe tomorrow would be better.

# 12 *The Scarecrows Arrive*

The rain lashed down without a break next day and although we trekked right through from dawn to dusk we managed to cover only eight miles. The jungle now seemed openly hostile, and I felt depressed. Hunger had driven me to break my family's trust and Father's harsh words had been wounding. But I could live with that. What I could not deal with were the shock waves of the Chinese ambush. The jolly *Boy's Own* picture of my family had been soiled by harsh adult realities – and I did not like it.

Darkness eventually forced us to stop for the night. After several futile attempts to get a fire going, we ate some cold rice and huddled together on the wet ground like a pack of wild animals. There was no shelter and we were too tired to do anything about it. When the swarms of mosquitoes, midges and leeches descended on us we did nothing – the effort was too much. It was tempting to give up the struggle and let go when you were on the edge of survival: but it was dangerous.

During the night the shivering bouts which had affected Maisie all day developed into violent ague accompanied by profuse sweating. There was no doubt at all about the diagnosis: Maisie was suffering from malaria. Poor sister, she could never swallow pills, capsules, castor oil, or anything remotely resembling medicine. When we had to queue outside the Major's surgery at home for a massive jab of the Mixture of the Day, she would become more and more hysterical until Father told her to clear off.

Now retribution had finally caught up with the offender. The restless influenza-like symptoms had given way to full-blown malaria. We had all swallowed quinine tablets every day for a month but Maisie had hidden hers. In fact, this treatment was not necessarily effective against the malignant malaria parasites in the swamps of the Hukawng.

We rose at dawn and set off along the jungle track in the pouring rain. Seven miles on we reached a stream of clean water, but conditions in the jungle were so bad that it took us twelve gruelling hours to cover the distance. Reasonably clean water was a rarity because the Chinese dead were piled up on the banks of rivers and streams, contaminating much of the water supply with cholera, dysentery, typhoid and other horrors. Of course our water was always boiled, but it was sensible to begin with something that did not contain parts of a Chinese soldier.

Our reserves of energy were beginning to reach their limit. Most of the time I was up to my thighs in clinging mud that seemed to have immense powers of suction. The heavy flask of water, which I hugged with both arms like a baby, meant that I could not stick my arms out to keep my balance. But, after my performance with the tin of milk-powder, I knew that if I dropped the flask in the mud I would be hanged from the nearest tree.

The adults suffered too, and I watched helplessly while Mum wept with frustration as she floundered knee-deep in the mud, one hand holding her longyi up, the other clutching her bag. Beside her, Father was bent almost double with the effort of dragging himself and Georgie forward. They stumbled and swayed, locked in their private battle against the elements. Close behind them came Maisie, clearly very ill as she lurched down the track with wild disjointed steps.

For a moment it seemed to me that the struggle was pointless. Yet every step was a victory for survival and a step nearer to India. Sometimes it was impossible to move more than a yard without stopping to allow our will-power to assert itself again for the next assault on the track. Rotting, foul-smelling corpses were everywhere but now the strength to make a detour round them had gone, so we stumbled over them. Every mile was a nightmare. Seven miles was a season in hell.

That evening we lay down on the ground in the rain, physically and mentally spent. As night fell Father began to shiver and sweat.

'I've got malaria, Puss,' he said to Mum.

So there it was. With Maisie sick we might have managed by taking turns to support her while we trekked. But with Father down as well, the trek was effectively over. His words echoed in my mind like a mocking bird: 'Remember, if you are sick I will leave you behind, because we cannot risk the lives of the others for the sake of one person.'

Was it really only a few days since I had shivered as this sentence of death was passed upon me? What an irony that this decision should now be in my hands. Yet surely it could not be right. Rules, discipline and army regulations had their place. But what about the bond of love? Did it matter? I should know. For, as my father had bidden me, I could now recite every verse of 1 Corinthians, chapter 13 without hesitation. The last line seemed to have a hollow ring in view of our current misfortune, yet I remember the inner strength it gave me, though, young as I was, I did not fully understand it: 'And now abideth faith, hope, love, these three; but the greatest of these is love.'

How strange that my father should have chosen his youngest child to memorise this chapter at a time when all seemed lost. Did he intend it as a spiritual survival kit that would get me through the years of turmoil ahead? Perhaps so, for the words still resonate in my mind.

However, the immediate question that faced us was: could we really leave Father and Maisie in the jungle while Mum, George and I walked on to India? Of course not. For me it was never an option. But if we stayed here until they died, would we ourselves be too sick to continue? Everything we had seen in the last month told us that if a family stopped for one member, the whole family died. We had passed too many families lying side by side, all dead under one blanket, to doubt that.

We were too tired to work out a solution that night. Perhaps things might be better tomorrow. They usually were on a bright sunny morning. Miracles, as far as I knew, were never performed at night.

But I was wrong.

My irrepressible childish banter always surfaced on a fine morning. 'Good-morning Father, Mum, Maisie, Georgie. Look! Leeches between my toes. Maisie, there's one up your skirt – Ha! Ha! What's for breakfast Mum? Don't tell me, I'll guess – rice ball and tea. Lovely. Hey! Georgie, there's a leech hanging out of your ear. Must have eaten your brains.'

'Shut up, Stevie, just shut up, will you.'

'Oh all right'.

Our two sick members were well enough to trek so we set out in good heart. By mid-morning we had made such steady progress that we could afford to enjoy an extended 'coffee break' of weak tea. I noticed with mild interest that Mum was smoking so many of her rolled 'tea cigarettes' that we would soon need a family committee meeting to decide whether we were going to smoke or drink the remaining tea-leaves.

As we ambled back to the footpath from our glade in the jungle we passed another dying Chinese soldier. He lay sprawled half-way across the track and it was clear that he would not see the treeless hills of Yunnan again. His eyes had sunk into his head and he was filthy. We passed him by with scarcely a glance – he was just one more dying refugee. But this one raised his head, struggled to lift himself on to one elbow and with his other hand he tapped his open mouth. A forlorn sign for food? Water? But we carried on walking.

Bringing up the rear, I staggered past with my penance, the heavy flask of water. I stared at the dying Chinese with no feeling of sympathy whatever. 'Serves you right,' I thought. 'Your lot ambushed us and made us suffer. Now it's your turn – how do you like it now you swine?'

What followed next has inspired me all my life. For Father stopped on the trail and said to us: 'That Chinese soldier is about to die. We cannot go past without giving him some water. We must go back.'

I could not believe it. Only a couple of days ago our lives had hung by a thread because of these thugs. The memory of the violence, the terror and the humiliation of Mum and Maisie was fresh in my mind. As Father argued with us, the black demons of revenge began to beat against my temples. 'Let the bastard die. Let the bastard die.'

The quarrel was bitter but after a few minutes we reluctantly gave way. Sullen and ungracious, we followed him back to the dying man. When we reached the soldier Father said, 'Stephen, give him some water.'

Controlling my anger with the greatest difficulty, I poured the water into the metal lid of the flask, Father held the soldier's head up and let him drink. Then he put the man's discarded bag under his head so that he was more comfortable. I turned away with the others to continue our journey. But we became aware that Father was still squatting beside the soldier and saying something to him. The dying man watched him with dark, tired eyes. His face was relaxed, almost serene. I knew my father was praying.

'The Lord is my shepherd; I shall not want ... he maketh me to lie down in green pastures ... yea, though I walk through the valley of the shadow of death, I will fear no evil for Thou art with me . . .'

How foolish, how absurd my childish anger seemed now in the face of my father's humility. I am sure the soldier sensed the compassion in the unintelligible foreign words recited by a stranger. I am glad he died in peace.

As for me, I realised that I had misjudged my father, for he was a bigger man than I could ever have imagined. Even in his darkest hour he struggled to keep faith with his God and his Christian beliefs.


By the afternoon of that day, 19 June, we were ten miles from our starting point of the morning. Another two miles and we would stop for the night. Then without warning disaster struck.

As we pushed our way through an area of particularly dense undergrowth, we came across a party of Gurkhas sheltering in a small clearing hidden by clumps of bamboo. They were in a state of considerable agitation, the women and children clustering around two inert bodies on the grass while the men had fanned out to take up positions over-looking the track. Each was armed with an army .303 rifle and it was clear they were looking for a fight.

We stood still so as not to alarm them but they beckoned to us urgently. '*Aao Sahib,*' they called out. '*Vahan mut jao. Chini budmarsh vahan hein.*' (Come Sir! Don't go there. The Chinese trouble-makers are there.) Intrigued, we hurried to join them.

They told us that about half-an-hour earlier, when they were several miles further up the track, a gang of Chinese bandits had sprung an ambush on them. Fearing for their women and children the Gurkhas decided to fight. There were several casualties on both sides, the battle subsiding only when the Gurkhas retreated back down the track to this hideout. They had carried two wounded companions back with them but left the dead behind. They were waiting here to collect enough refugees for a determined assault on the Chinese positions. Hence their joyful welcome when they saw us, despite the fact that our party consisted of a 70-year-old Major, his Burmese wife and three children, with an armoury of one silver-handled kukri between the five of us.

Father treated the wounded but after an hour, when we had been joined by only a small party of starving skeletons, he had had enough. He was always a man of action and waiting for things to happen exasperated him. So he made another of his controversial decisions.

There was no point in hanging about in the undergrowth any longer, he announced. The Chinese had probably gone so we might as well get going. After explaining this to the startled Gurkhas, he gathered his family about him and strode openly down the track. The fact that he was armed only with a pocket New Testament and an old army haversack did not dent his resolve. However young Stephen, his foolhardy son, who was armed with an offensive weapon – namely a Gurkha kukri – knew that when the bullets began to fly they would undoubtedly all be aimed at him.

It was now late in the afternoon and sunlight sliced through the tangle of tall trees in bars of orange light. It was a beautiful sight, the going was firm and our little party moved along at a leisurely pace. My flask was almost empty so I was able to walk well ahead of the others, my head full of dreams as the miles rolled by.

Eventually I arrived at a place where the thick tangle of forest gave way to a small open area of short grass. Wandering pensively through the centre of the glade, I noticed a body lying on the right-hand verge of the track. I would have ignored it except for the fact that it was a Gurkha and he had been shot several times.

Since I had never seen gun-shot wounds at such close quarters before, I studied the round bullet-holes curiously and I remember being surprised by the amount of dark dried blood that caked the body and the grass around. Like the other dead I had seen however, the Gurkha's open eyes stared at nothing and the familiar feeling of finality hung heavily in the air.

About twenty yards along the track I came across another body. It was that of a Chinese soldier. He was sprawled across the track with his arms splayed out beside him, looking lonely and abandoned like the Gurkha I had just seen. Without a moment's hesitation I stepped over him, in the accepted manner when confronted by a dead person on the track.

YYYYYAAAAAAAaaaahhhhhh! While my legs were astride the dead body it came to life! Jesus Christ All Bloody Mighty! A hand shot up and grabbed my silver key-chain. I thought I was having a heart attack. I could not move a muscle. I was not even sure if I was breathing. My eyeballs swivelled downwards, and I looked straight into the face of the Chinese soldier, who was staring back at me. Help! I thought I was going to pass out. My heart seemed to be racing in one continuous thundering beat. What was happening? My mind was blanked out. The face was still staring at me and I could hear it shouting. But I could not move and the hand still gripped my key chain. Oh bloody hell!

I do not know how long I stood astride the Chinese soldier. Perhaps it was several seconds. Even as I write this my palms begin to sweat, my heart gallops and I need a break. Strange, isn't it, how the power of a distant mental disturbance can bridge the years.

I was roused by a voice that echoed through the jungle: 'Stephen! Why have you stopped there? Come on boy! Get on with it will you. It's getting late.'

My father walked into my nightmare, thrusting an overhanging branch aside. Behind him came Mum, Maisie and Georgie. I wish I could have shouted a warning but my voice was not working. When I heard the crackle of dry leaves all around us I knew it was too late: we were in the middle of an ambush. The soldier playing dead on the path had been the bait. Now the trap-door was about to close.

This time they did not bawl at us or fling our possessions around like the louts at the last encounter. This was a classic ambush and a lot more sinister. My family hurried to my side as the 'dead' Chinese got up, ripped my key-chain off my belt and flourished a loaded pistol in our faces. A quick glance at the jungle was enough to warn us that we were surrounded by a large group of fully-armed Chinese soldiers who remained partly hidden in the scrub that bordered the glade. An armed officer and half-a-dozen soldiers stepped out and came towards us.

Our hands went up as the guns prodded us. We knew the drill now. Father went up to the officer and explained that he was an officer also and that this was his family. I think the man understood some English because there were sharp exchanges but no thumps and threats this time. I think Father gave the man some money and I have a faint recollection that his gold pocket-watch and chain were taken. They also took the last remains of our rice and the thermos flask before crowding around Mum and Maisie. Someone wanted to see what Mum was carrying and began to maul her. This was going to end very badly in another minute. All those jewels round her waist!

Father quickly intervened, showing them in sign language that his wife was very sick. She was old and had a bad stomach problem. The yelling began afresh.

'*Eee orr. Eee orr. Eee orr.*' What the blazes were they saying?

There was that tight feeling in my chest again. Would they rip my kukri off my waist? Should I be passive, even cowardly, and let them take it or should I shout, just once, 'You stinking bandits!'

Mum gave me a long stare as if to say, 'Don't do anything stupid Stevie.'

Meanwhile, Father tried to persuade the officer to let us go. In any case the Chinese must have realised by now from our rags and the small quantity of rice we were carrying that we were totally destitute. The truth was that we were in a worse state than these bandits – except for the jewels. Finally the men were called off and the officer indicated that we were free to leave.

We shuffled down the track in our bare feet, mortified by the shame of our submission once again. My elegant Mum:

old with stomach problems? Indeed! But such insults were included in the price of survival. Oh Lindfield, Lindfield!

And so we went on our way. In the twilight we noticed that the jungle was thinning out and the path we were on had widened into a muddy cart-track. Before long we caught a glimpse of dilapidated huts and Naga longhouses through the trees. Beyond them an open field of grass stretched to the banks of a river. And beyond the river the land began to rise in successive ridges, higher and higher until the furthest of them was hidden by banks of swirling monsoon clouds.

Perhaps our minds were dulled by fatigue and lack of food, because the significance of what we were seeing did not register. Turning off the track we settled on a patch of damp earth, lit a fire and huddled round it while Mum boiled a pan of jungle greens for supper. Darkness had fallen when the Gurkhas we had met earlier emerged from the jungle and settled on the grass not far away. A distraught woman with them began to wail in a most distressing way. In the silence of the night her voice had an intensity that was almost unbearable.

'*Kanchi, kanchi,*' she cried. '*Kanchi, kanchi, kanchi.*'

Again and again, hour after hour. It was clear her loved one had been killed by the Chinese and nothing could comfort her.

'*Kanchi, kanchi.*'

My fists were clenched as I tried desperately to blot out the picture of another woman, at another time, grieving for her son. But I lost the battle and the memory came flooding in.

'Richard. Richard. My son. Please God, not Richard.'

Asian women weeping without restraint for their men. Perhaps it had always been so. Men killing men because they were not content with what they had. And women left to weep over their lifeless bodies. I wish I could forget. But how do you do it? A stiff upper lip? Well yes, the Major would have preferred that. But in the stillness of the night, when the cherry trees start to bloom and the voices call, what then, my friend?

Next morning we walked into the village where a glance at the scenery beyond the river confirmed the scale of our achievement. Those green hills towering before us were the Patkoi hills. Somewhere up there among the crests was the Pangsau pass, over 4,000 feet high. And beyond it was India.

This view could only mean that we had passed through the Valley of Death, yet strangely there was barely a flicker of elation on our faces. We were tired and hungry and those ridges looked daunting, especially when the monsoon clouds swept ominously across them. The fighting spirit and the courage were still there but the physical strength had gone. Our recent experience had taught us that to survive an enterprise like this we needed both physical and mental strength. However great our will to survive, if we had to crawl, we were finished.

Yet we had plenty to be proud of. According to Maisie's diary we were 293 miles from our starting point at Myitkyina, having overcome every obstacle in our path: swollen rivers, swamps, starvation, disease and Chinese bandits. Sleeping on the ground, in the rain, without shelter. Dressed in rags, with nothing left but our pride, we had made it.

But blocking our path to India still was the southern extension of the Himalayan mountain chain. In its valleys flowed many rivers which were doubtless in spate, while above them stretched successive rows of steep ridges. It was going to be very tough, but if we could make a dash for India now, what an achievement it would be. What a story to tell our people – a trek from Myitkyina to India in the teeth of the south-west monsoon!

Later, when we asked the name of this village we were told it was called Shingbwiyang.

Shingbwiyang? At the time it meant nothing to us.

# 13   *Shingbwiyang*

Next morning we learned something incredible. The official from the Burma Frontier Service who was responsible for this territory was based in Shingbwiyang. His name was Clive North – the very man who had recently been a guest at our home in Maymyo. Given the state of our undernourished brains, this information had the same destabilising effect on us as the mental wallop that Livingstone must have felt when Stanley walked into his camp. It seemed too good to be true. We had been too often disappointed on this journey to take such good tidings too seriously. But all our doubts were dissipated when several of the inhabitants confirmed to Father that this was indeed the Clive North we knew. Our spirits rose. Without further hesitation, we set out to meet our old acquaintance.

About a quarter-of-a-mile from the village we climbed a small hill to where a pleasant wooden bungalow and some outbuildings stood in a clearing. Rather ominously a stout bamboo fence surrounded the compound and an armed sentry guarded the single gate. He watched us approach with growing agitation, alarmed by our filthy appearance and tattered clothes. But Father brushed him aside and strode purposefully towards the front door of the bungalow. We followed as meekly as we could, for we had looked down too many gun barrels in the last few days. However, there was no hail of bullets as Father confidently climbed the stairs and entered the bungalow, leaving the four of us outside.

We sat on the ground, overwhelmed by a sense of deliverance, not daring to speak in case the act unsettled our good fortune. In my childish imagination the picture of North staring in disbelief at the dirty vagabond who looked vaguely like his friend Major Brookes of Lindfield amused me no end. What a reunion this would be. They would have so many things to discuss, like the route to India, food supplies, the fate of Willie and the orphan girls, and more. For about twenty minutes we gazed at the view, breathing in the sense of peace after our weeks of anguish in the jungle. We felt safe at last.

But we were mistaken, for suddenly we were shaken out of our reverie by the sound of strident voices from the bungalow. They grew louder by the second. Unbelievably it sounded like a serious quarrel. Father's voice roared above the general rumble. I knew that sound – the Major was angry. All thoughts of peace vanished. We struggled to our feet, instinctively clinging to Mum for reassurance and protection. Abruptly the commotion in the house was replaced by the sound of Father's feet thumping the wooden floor as he strode towards the front door. Then he flung it open and stormed down the stairs. His voice was heavy with bitterness.

'Come on, let's go,' was all he said.

We hobbled after him as he marched out of the compound, straight past the startled sentry and down towards the village. Past experience warned me that a careless question at this stage was like throwing gunpowder on a fire. So I held my peace and as a result I never found out exactly what happened in North's house. I'm sure Mum and Maisie were told eventually, but I had to rely on my intuition to build a picture of this encounter.

I suppose we should have realised, from our experiences over the past few months, that the only unfailing source of strength and support when the chips were down was the family. Strangers and friends could be helpful but they had their limits. Only the bond of blood was strong enough to withstand the pressure of self-interest when the going was tough.

And so I believe it was with North. I do not suppose my father expected, or even asked, for special treatment. Perhaps he pleaded that urgent help be sent to Willie and the orphans. Maybe he asked for food and shelter for his family for a couple of days. After all, there was really nothing else in the gift of North that my father needed. But if he turned away someone he knew, during the worst stages of that terrible trek, it seems unforgivable, particularly when accompanied by shouts and argument.

I like to think that my mother's Burmese origins had nothing to do with what happened. But the British Empire of over half-a-century ago was riddled with racial prejudice. Of course there were many enlightened men and women whose lives were enriched by the experience of living in Asia, as a huge body of literature attests. But for some the transition from a subordinate position in England to ruling some distant city or province was a step too far in self-regard. Unhappily, being Anglo-Burmese, I was sensitive to the behaviour of both races — an uncomfortable state to be in at the best of times.

The outcome of the meeting with North effectively killed our hopes of reaching India. The civil and military authorities had made the decision to close the route. The entry in Maisie's diary simply states: 'Ordered not to leave Shingbwiyang till the end of the rains and till further orders issued.' It was a defining moment that changed the fortunes of our family.

I discovered later that a British group had escaped along the same route we took. The party of seventeen, which included the ADC to the Governor of Burma and two servants, was led by the Deputy High Commissioner of Myitkyina. They had funds to hire bearers to carry their baggage and medicines when they crossed the Kumon range. At Maingkwan, the village where we left our Gurkha companions, they bought bullocks to replace the bearers for their baggage train. When they reached Shingbwiyang they restocked with food, no doubt from North's supplies, then set out across the Patkoi Hills and reached India on 10 June. The Deputy High Commissioner, who had left the party at the ferry on the Tarung river where he stopped to help the Indian Civil Service official who was operating it, passed through Shingbwiyang on about 15 June. He arrived in India on

25 June. We, on the other hand, who had reached
Shingbwiyang on 19 June, were prevented from leaving the
village.

Our shelter in Shingbwiyang was a traditional Naga longhouse. It was a barn-like building, about fifty feet long,
with a wood and bamboo frame, thatched walls and a floor
of split bamboo stems. The thatched roof extended several
feet beyond the walls to give some protection from the rain.
I do not remember any windows, but there was a door at
either end which opened into a long corridor that ran the
length of the building, splitting it into two halls. These halls
were the communal living quarters which the Naga families – the young and the old – happily shared with their pets
and chickens. Finally, to protect it from ground water
during the monsoon and from prowling enemies and predators, the whole building was perched on wooden stilts
about five feet off the ground. Entry to this human beehive
was via a log with footholds cut into it.

Our longhouse was one of a cluster of four. They stood
at the edge of a large meadow with thick jungle on three
sides. The boundary on the fourth side was formed by a
small river which wandered southwards through the jungle
to join up with a tributary of the Chindwin. Within this
open space the Nagas must have celebrated their festivals
and tended their crops, until the arrival of the diseased refugees made them flee for their lives. A short distance from
the longhouses, several brand-new huts had been built to
accommodate the steady influx of people as the monsoon
intensified. In all there were about a dozen huts and

long–houses forming a community of civilians and troops.

In the distance, fringed by the river, were the huts of the Chinese Fifth Army, separated from us by the no–man's-land of the meadow. We viewed their collection of huts nervously for the Chinese would pour out of them like locusts when the supply planes dropped sacks of food for us. Although their officers tried to stop them by beating them with sticks and even shooting them, the soldiers would fight for the food, ripping open the sacks and making off with the contents.

These two hamlets, together with the rice godowns and Clive North's house on the hill, made up the village of Shingbwiyang. But for the Japanese invasion of Burma, few people apart from Clive North and the Nagas would have known of its existence. But a terrible fate was in store for these luckless villagers, for by 1942 construction had already begun of a road from India, which would cut through their forests and hills to link up with the Burma Road from China. It was called the Ledo Road after the town in India where the road began. The twentieth century was about to arrive with a vengeance, replacing the Nagas' arrows and ancient shotguns with planes, tanks and artillery in the space of twelve months.

We could smell our longhouse from a long way off. When we climbed the log stairs and entered the dark corridor we realised why – there was a dead body lying in it. It was covered with flies and must have lain there for at least two days. Holding our breath, we inched past, stepping gingerly over fly-infested fluids. Horrified, we shuffled along the corridor until we came to two doors, one to the left and one to the right. With Father leading, we turned right into a long hall which ran the length of the building.

It took a few moments for our eyes to adjust to the murky interior. Then we saw them – people, lots of them, crammed together. Probably a hundred, maybe more, all lying down on squares of hessian sacking made from discarded rice bags. Some had fires going, but as there were no chimneys the smoke drifted up and spread along the length of the hall, adding to the gloom. Voices could be heard, rambling or calling, but no-one replied. And the place stank – of human excreta, of rotting bodies and infected sores, and of putrid food and waste. Swarms of flies were everywhere. It was like a scene from Dante's *Inferno*. This must be what hell looked and smelt like. There was no human dignity here: these people were like cows or chickens in a cage, lying in their own dirt. I knew for certain that God was not present. I have never felt so low or so despairing.

Thankfully Father did not falter. He led us past the figures on the floor to a space at the far end of the hall where parts of the bamboo wall had rotted away. Although the monsoon rain flooded in when there was a high wind, it was a small price to pay for fresh air and light. Even more important, we could gaze out of this place and restore our sanity by recognising that there was still another world outside.

We lay down on the bamboo floor with our heads against the outer wall. I lay between Georgie and Maisie. Strangely enough, I could think of nothing. My mind was like a black void through which things flashed but never stopped long

enough to be recognisable. I remember feeling very frightened and lying absolutely still so as not to attract the
attention of the delirious invalids around me.

Meanwhile Father had lit a fire on the hearth-stones and
in a short time Mum had boiled some water for a welcome
cup of tea. Yet although the firelight dispersed the ghosts
from my imagination, the oppressive feeling of doom still
bore down on me. I felt a menace within the longhouse that
I had not experienced before, even when we were sleeping
in the darkness of the jungle. Perhaps the stark realisation
that we could be stuck in this apalling asylum for weeks,
even months, had something to do with it. After weeks of
crashing through the jungle I had become used to living in
the open. Struggling against the rain, the mud and the
mountains had been a reason for living. But this place was
a prison filled with sadness. I crept into the middle of our
family group and clung desperately to Mum like a drowning child.

'*Nah-leh-thee tha. Nah-leh-thee,*' she whispered. ('I understand, son. I understand.')

It took several minutes for my racing mind to slow down.
Then the madness began to drain away and the fighting
spirit asserted itself again. But I was never at ease in the
longhouse and twinges of fear would run through me when
I least expected it.

When my eyes grew accustomed to the faint reflected
light, I noticed that not more than a couple of yards from
us was an Indian family. The husband, wife and five children lay in a line on pieces of sacking placed against the wall
of the central corridor. They studied us with wide, staring
eyes. None of them uttered a word. Suddenly I understood

the meaning of those strange looks: we were occupying the space left by people who had recently died. These stained hessian sacks we were lying on were probably saturated with germs from their remains.

I realised too that there would be no privacy in the grisly process of dying, for next to this family lay an Anglo-Indian man who was clearly ill with malaria from the way he was shaking. He had wrapped himself in a blanket and some old hessian sacks with just his face protruding from the bundle. It was too dark to see much beyond him. On our wall, next to Maisie, was another Anglo-Indian who seemed to slip in and out of delirium and clearly enjoyed talking to himself, even when he seemed to have his wits about him.

This, then, was the place which from May to October 1942 was the gateway to India for about 45,000 refugees and Chinese soldiers. Most of them died in the village, others died on the track to India, but no one cares any more. It was merely a side-show in the great scheme of things.

Within a few days I began to make forays into the jungle in search of bamboo shoots and edible plants. On the off-chance that I might meet Naga or Kachin villagers prepared to sell food, Mum gave me three silver coins to finance my transactions. I knew nothing of trade or high finance, but I bubbled with excitement at the prospect of a cooked dinner. Fired up like this, I was moving along a narrow path one day when I came across a Naga man digging up a clump of wild ginger. Instantly two silver coins changed hands and the bunch was mine. Proud of my business skills I ran back to the longhouse and presented Mum with my purchase. I still giggle when I remember the quizzical look on her face. Words were unnecessary for her eyes said it all: 'What's this? No eggs? No chickens? What the hell am I supposed to do with wild ginger Stevie? Ginger stew? Roast ginger? Any ideas?'

But she was sweet and we laughed about it – until we had plain ginger and rice for dinner. I never went trading again.

As it happened, we were soon introduced to a more sophisticated method of procuring food. It was a day when nothing stirred in the longhouse, for the oppressive heat and high humidity seemed to drain every ounce of energy from the inmates. In our corner the five of us dozed, lying uneasily on three blankets which Father said he had 'found' next door. I guessed what that meant, but I was past caring as long as they were not teeming with maggots from the body. Suddenly a shuddering rumble shook the hut as something passed overhead. Japanese planes? I needed no second warning and before the others could even sit up, I had dived through the mat wall, slipped down a bamboo support-pole and was sprinting for the jungle.

Minutes later I heard the sound again. Could it really be a Dakota? I ran out into the open. Stone the crows! There it was, coming in low over the tree-tops. The round nose, high tail and two engines emitting that glorious sound that always set my pulse racing. What a sight! It was following a course that would take it straight across the meadow in the centre of the village.

Then I saw it – no side door! Twitching with nerves I yelled instinctively: 'No side door, mate. Look out, the side door's open.'

As I watched in awe, the plane flashed past about 150 feet

above the ground, while sacks poured out of the open door. Crikey! It was raining sacks of food. Down they came like bombs, at high speed, probably a dozen of them, striking the meadow in huge sprays of stagnant water, then bounding up into the air again. Three more bounces, gentler than the first, one burst sack spewing rice and bully beef tins as it rose for the last time, before they all slithered to a stop in the long grass. The note of the Dakota engines changed abruptly to a shuddering roar as the pilot slammed the throttles wide open and heaved the nose up to clear the trees which lined the far perimeter. I watched open-mouthed as the plane banked to the left, gained height and swung round in a wide circle ready for the next pass. The whole performance left me weak-kneed and breathless.

For the first time in my life I was witnessing an air-drop, a modern miracle in which gods showered food from the skies. But my astonishment was nothing compared to the impact this had on the Nagas. Behind me the jungle rustled and snapped as they bolted en masse into the sanctuary of the forest, for here was witchcraft. Thus are legends born – of giant eagles, of men who flew and of the mythical Garuda Bird which swooped down from the heavens and laid its eggs in the green meadow of Shingbwiyang.

People began to pour out of our huts and the Chinese huts, fighting for possession of the sacks. A Chinese officer fired a pistol, others wielded sticks. I could hardly believe what I was watching. By this time a dull rumble should have warned the contestants that the plane was on the way for another drop, but they were too busy. Then the sacks were bouncing over the meadow, skipping and splashing like huge cannon-balls. Most people dived out of the way, but the Chinese ignored the danger. They were so hungry that they cut the sacks open on the field and made off with the rice, stuffing it into pockets, bags, bits of cloth, tins, anything that would hold it. Our team returned to the fray when the plane had passed, dragging their spoils towards our huts.

The plane made half-a-dozen passes before it peeled off to the west. Fascinated, I watched it circling as it gained height to clear the high ridges of the Patkoi Hills and receded into the distance. Around me people continued to argue and fight but I had lost interest.

Shortly after this it came to our ears that those who went out during a supply-drop and carried the heavy sacks of food up to North's godowns received an extra ration of rice and goodies. So that was how the system worked. Even more interesting to us were the packets of biscuits and tins of squashed bully-beef and cheese that people had smuggled in their clothing from the sacks which had burst open. This aroused our survival instincts to the extent that Father decided to take me down to the next supply-drop so we could collect an extra ration of rice. I felt so proud. I was 11 years old and all the other handlers were men, yet my father trusted me to do this job.

And so about a fortnight later, when the sound of the Dakota had the handlers sprinting for the meadow, Father and I were in the forefront. But when I stood in the open, looking across at the line of trees and the black-winged shape hurtling towards me, I was not so sure this was a good idea. But it was too late, for even as I heard Father yell 'Keep close to me, Stephen,' the sky was filled with whirling sacks. I saw six large tumbling objects coming straight for me at a hundred miles an hour, so fast I had time for one decision only – dodge the first one and pray that the others flew past unaccompanied by bits of my body. Unusually for me, I was so confused that I froze like a rabbit, while the sacks bounced and whizzed beside me and over me. I had no doubt that if one hit me I would be killed stone dead.

At this stage Father realised it had been a mistake to bring me with him. While the plane was lining up for the next pass, he grabbed me by the arm and led me away from the dropping zone. Although I protested loudly, even I knew that my performance with the high-speed sacks was unconvincing. I made myself very small and hid in the grass so as not to tempt Fate.

When it was all over I tried to lift a sack but it would not budge. It was probably three times my own weight or more. However, to avoid letting the side down, I found a burst sack with its contents scattered over a wide area and carried some of the rice in a piece of hessian up to North's godown with Father and the others. My presence raised some eyebrows but I got my rations anyway and returned home in triumph.

Later, when no one was looking, I passed Mum a packet of hard biscuits, some squashed bully beef and a handful of tea-leaves that I had hidden in my clothes. How she laughed. But Father never asked me to help during a food drop again. It was a relief, for there were enough other ways of dying in the Hukawng.

# 14  The Longhouse of Tears

Any official worth his salt would have known that confinement in the germ-infested longhouses was surely death. It did not take much intelligence to work that out. The first to go was a daughter of the Indian family opposite us. The whole family were listless and gaunt, but on the scale of scarecrow classification I would have put their chances of survival at about the same as ours – namely twenty per cent.

We had the first inkling that something was wrong with agitated cries from the mother in the darkness before dawn. They went on for several minutes and I confess that I put my hands over my ears. Then, just when it seemed all was well, the mother let out a piercing scream. I had no idea what was going on although she was only a few feet away from us.

The wailing gradually grew in intensity until the rafters echoed with her cry, the maniacal Asian variety that gripped my stomach in a vice and loosened the hinges of my mind. We all knew for sure that another life had ended, yet around her, all was silent. No one called out or moved to help, though in the bleak obscurity of night, several pairs of weary eyes must have been open, watchful for the icy touch of death that would bring their own release from pain and suffering.

But the woman's torment had only just begun. Her husband and her three remaining daughters all died within the space of a few days and she spiralled downwards into a mental breakdown. Her plight was made worse by the camp administration, run by North, which left her for several days with two dead children beside her because no one was available to bury them.

After her last daughter died the distraught mother tried to remove the girl's earrings, but the child had been dead for over a day and this was difficult. So the mother sliced the girl's earlobes off with a pair of scissors and extracted the earrings. The memory of that poor insane mother violating her dead daughter's body in this way still makes me shudder with pity and horror.

Only one child of this family remained, a little boy of about six. He developed a sore on the back of his head, near the base of his skull, which, because of the filthy conditions in the longhouse, was crawling with maggots within a week. We wept for him as he squealed and twitched in agony. Just remembering it again makes me sad and angry. What was this nonsense about God's love and compassion if it permitted something like this?

As for the boy, my father patiently sat behind him for an hour or more every day, carefully removing the maggots with tweezers and swabbing the wound with kerosene.

Despite the lack of anaesthetics, the boy endured the daily probing and plugging of the hole with scarcely a whimper. By now Father himself was seriously ill with malaria but he never missed a session. In due course his persistence paid off; the wound healed and the boy recovered.

The Anglo-Indian man next to this family had also developed an open 'Naga sore' on his shin about three inches in diameter. But Father got to it before the flies, and like the boy, the man survived.

But the doctor who had performed miracles on others would soon have to perform one on himself and on his own daughter if they were to survive, for within the bloodstream of them both the malaria parasites were multiplying fast. The shivering, profuse sweating, ice-cold skin and joint pains they had at first suffered infrequently were now a regular occurrence. They were the warning signs that a crisis was approaching, yet the only drug we had to hold the infection in check was quinine.

Further down the hall towards the opening in the corridor others were also suffering and dying, but I avoided going that way. There was enough misery in our corner to last me a lifetime. I always went out through the hole in our wall and slid down an angled log which served as stairs. Then I would wander alone through the forest, looking at the strange trees, flowers and butterflies or hunting for edible plants, until my racing mind calmed down.

On my way back I always rested on an old log by the stream which flowed past our longhouse, so that I could dream of the halcyon days without the smell of rotting human bodies in my nose. Sometimes when the rain-clouds parted I could see a Naga village, much like ours, high up on the slopes of the Patkoi Hills, and once I saw a Dakota carrying out a supply-drop over it which implied that friendly forces were in residence.

I was sitting here one day when a peculiar aircraft with a radial engine, fixed wheels and high wings like a dragonfly emerged from the murky hills. I watched it circle the meadow a few times before it released a package attached to a white streamer. 'Ah! Mr North's lunch no doubt, and the morning papers for the others,' I guessed. It probably contained instructions and money from India for the man who lived on the hill who, I might add, had not set foot in these huts since our arrival.

While the plane continued its leisurely circuits of the village, a number of people emerged from the direction of the hill and began to scrabble about in the meadow. Intrigued, I watched as they hurriedly erected two tall bamboo poles about twenty feet apart which were linked at the top by a loop of stout cord. From this loop hung what looked like a leather pouch.

By this time the plane, which I discovered was called a Lysander, was coming in very low across the meadow. As it passed me I saw a metal rod with a hook protruding from below the fuselage, just behind the wheels, and realised that the pilot's task was to snatch the cord as he flew past. This he succeeded in doing after three attempts. The pouch was drawn into the aircraft and it turned towards the west, hurrying home before the storm closed in. Dreaming on my perch, I wondered if a true picture of the crisis at Shingbwiyang was ever carried back in those parcels.

By this stage, Maisie's diary entries had shrunk to single words like 'rain' or an occasional 'heavy rain' and a rare 'no rain'. She had made no entry for 27 June but I had written in my childish handwriting: 'Stevie's Birthday'. I forgive her for the omission, but Father decided to do something special for me, though how he arranged and paid for it I cannot say. It began with a loud report from a rifle, just behind our hut, followed by a brief squealing sound. Soon Mum turned up with half-a-side of suckling pig which she roasted on the embers of our open fire. Oh! the scent of nectar, of real food, wafted in the air. A large succulent chunk on a banana leaf was given to me as a birthday present by my father. When I tore off a fat, juicy piece with my bare fingers and popped it in my mouth, I wept. A tide of suppressed emotions swept away my self-control and for the first time in many months I cried without restraint in front of my family.

It was not just the sheer bliss of tasting roasted meat again; nor the powerful communal feeling of having my family sitting round this fire with me, destitute and ill though they were. These were certainly part of it. But most of all it was to do with the affirmation of my father's and mother's unbroken fidelity and love for their children. I could see it in their actions and hear it in their voices and I have never forgotten it. I would not claim that this was the finest meal I have ever had, but for me it was the most emotional and powerful. It also marked the end of my childhood, for I was 12 now and very soon there would be man's work to be done.

A few days later the condition of Maisie's neighbour began to deteriorate. The old man was delirious for long periods and had difficulty with eating and keeping clean. Since Maisie was unwell and could not stand the rambling any longer, my parents decided we should change places. I tried to stay calm as I lay next to him but it was bad, especially at night. Some nights he scared the hell out of me, but when he spoke to his relatives and friends it made me sad. He also had long conversations with people from the Bible. The night he died he was mumbling as usual in the dark when suddenly, in a strong, clear voice, he said with genuine affection: 'Hello, Jesus. I've been waiting for you.'

Now for me at the age of 12, the idea of seeing Jesus flying around with a host of angels holding trumpets was impressive – in theory. But when it came to the real thing, hovering over a dying man, beside me, at midnight, in a headhunter's longhouse, in the Valley of Death, it was more than my courage could take. Hardly daring to breathe, I tried to slide slowly towards Maisie but I was too scared of attracting attention, so I shut my eyes very tightly instead. In the meantime, the old man's conversation with the spectre continued on and off for several minutes, and as the intervals grew longer I dropped off to sleep. Early next morning I sat up and looked in his direction. But I already knew that he was dead. What a sad and lonely end for an old man, with only a terrified boy for company.

Problems with burials had become critical as the death rate touched fifty a day. This meant 350 dead bodies every seven days. It was North's job to organise the burial parties, but too often they were unable to keep up with the work, particularly when the monsoon intensified and the village became like a lake dwelling. Consequently dead bodies lay where they were, exposed to the hot and humid atmosphere, rotting and smelling for days. It was gruesome, totally unacceptable, and bad for morale. Worse, it encouraged the spread of diseases which we were trying to control with the limited range of medicines available.

When the military and civil authorities decided to stop the westward movement of refugees they failed to provide adequate support to deal with the consequences of that decision. It is futile to argue that more would have died if they had been free to continue their trek to India supported by air drops of food, because this was never put to the test.

July came, with high winds chasing vast swathes of grey cloud that stretched from the sky down to the tree-tops of the jungle. Occasionally the wind won and blue skies appeared above us. Yes, *blue* skies – startling after the perpetual shroud of grey. Even the gloom of the diary lifts for a moment with the entry 'beautiful sunshine'. Our spirits rose so recklessly that Maisie and I decided to trot down to the meadow and take part in the sacred ritual of an air-drop. We were motivated by one idea: extra rations!

With Mum's cry of 'Be careful, you two' ringing in our ears, we left the longhouse by the tree-trunk staircase and headed, hand-in-hand, to where, by some miraculous modern hocus-pocus, sacks of food would fall from a passing iron bird. It was all very weird for me because Maisie was approaching the critical phase of malaria and was not the ideal companion when quick wits were vital. She could inconveniently go quite limp and dizzy and she rambled aimlessly for a lot of the time. I hoped desperately that she would not start hallucinating when faced with a dozen airborne sacks of rice. Having survived one air-drop with Father I felt reasonably confident of dodging them myself. But my sister presented a problem.

We stood in the knee-high grass with the other foolish human targets, chatting and passing the time of day in a most civilised manner. Now and again Maisie almost fainted but she recovered, blinked a few times, and continued the conversation we had had an hour ago, or even yesterday – behaviour that did nothing to calm my racing heart.

A sound like the faint beat of a distant drum was heard across the meadow. I knew that sound – and if I heard it today I would whisper to myself 'Dakota' and the years would fall away. I saw it, up on the flanks of the Patkoi ridge, cruising down effortlessly with its face to the wind. Its stubby nose reminded me of my childhood sweetheart, little June. Everything about that serene iron bird made me want to fly and swoop through the sky, clouds in my hair and the wind in my breath, free at last from this suffocating earth.

For a few moments it was lost behind the high trees on the far perimeter. Then with a roar that drowned out every other sound it came in, low, fast and dead ahead. The others saw it in an instant and ran to where they imagined the sacks would land, but my sister smiled and talked to me of our days at school. Oh dear! what a time to go cuckoo, Boozie. There was no point in running so I grinned and held her hand, but out of the corner of my eye I watched the iron bird fill the sky and sweep majestically over our heads with a deep-chested cry. The ground shook. Maisie chatted in happy delirium. I wished this was a dream. Suddenly dark shapes were in the air, tumbling, coming down fast, followed by thuds and swishing sounds as the heavy sacks of rice danced all around us. I was glad, and a little surprised, to find that we were still alive.

However, I knew this was merely a prelude. The real fun would begin during the next three passes when the crew unloaded the main cargo. That usually separated the men from the boys, or in our case, the sane from those of unsound mind. I was convinced that my nerves would not stand the strain of ignoring the flying sacks if Maisie went delirious. So with a little tact I urged her to help me retrieve a sack that had landed some way from the target area, and so we survived. Of course we could not move the sack between us, but we picked up some odds and ends and some spilt rice and made our way up to the house on the hill.

Our 'friend' on the hill was allocating grain like some latter-day Pharaoh to a bunch of scavenging Israelites. It was a far cry from Lindfield. Our portion was shovelled into a sack and I believe North said to Maisie, 'Pick it up.' Feverish and light-headed with malaria, she grabbed one end but pitched forward on to her face when she tried to lift it. I rushed up shouting, 'It's all right, Boozie. I'll help you. I can do it.' Gripping one end of the sack I heaved it on to my back. I may have been dressed in rags but one thing I never lost was my pride. My name was Brookes and I was as good as the best. We staggered back to the longhouse, resolved to keep silent about the incident. After all, my father had better things to think about.

Over the next two weeks the planes visited us twice, but each time the weather was so atrocious that the pilots decided to bomb us with our stores from a high altitude rather than risk the low level joy-ride. The first plane seemed to be droning aimlessly in the thick cloud above the village for over twenty minutes. Then suddenly there was a whooshing sound followed by an almighty bang and I saw a rectangular object falling at high speed through the clouds. It hit the ground with a loud thud. Some of us crept towards this thing, and were disappointed to find that it was a huge, folded tarpaulin which probably weighed several hundred pounds. One had hit the edge of a hut and plunged right through the roof and floor, embedding itself in the soil beneath. Hell's teeth! We were being bombed with giant tarpaulins. By the end of the day over a dozen of them had skewered Shingbwiyang. Weeks later we discovered these tarpaulins roofing the new huts for the survivors.

A few days later parachutes holding large crates floated down through the clouds. Was the government really sending us medicines? The drifting parachutes were fun to watch until one veered out of control and plunged into the jungle with a resounding crash. The precious medicines were squandered before they had saved a single life. When I saw another parachute twisting high above our longhouse, I raced into the undergrowth after it in my bare feet, and found the damaged crate. My family's survival was all I could think of, and I helped myself to what turned out to be some quinine tablets and some anti-mosquito cream before alerting the search-parties.

There was no doubt any more that Father and Maisie had lost the long battle with malaria. They began to drift in and out of consciousness with increasing regularity. We gave them what care and comfort we could. Mum remained strong, almost defiant, until poor Georgie began to fade. He did not seem to have a particular ailment, but just got physically weaker every day. Then I, who had avoided all major illnesses from the day we started our escape, suffered a violent attack of diarrhoea. By the third week of July, almost exactly three months since we had left our home in Maymyo, the Brookes clan was facing the real possibility of extinction.

The rain continued to pour down. The five of us lay silently side-by-side on the floor. Up to now I had always felt an inner strength, an assurance that ultimately my family would triumph. Now, for the first time, I felt this strength falter. 'Let it happen,' I thought. 'Blow it! I'm too tired to fight.'

But deep inside me an involuntary force seemed to stir and call out to me in my mother's voice, 'Stevie, get up. Come on. Get up, Stevie.' Within a few days I emerged from this defeatist phase. I was never ill again on the trek.

Father's violent ague now reached a crisis point: though blankets and sacks were piled on top of him, he still shivered and his skin felt cold and clammy. As the hours passed it was clear that he was fighting his last battle. The four of us crowded round him to give him some moral support and privacy. When he wanted to pass water we lifted him up so that he was kneeling, while Mum held an old sardine tin up to his thighs. The urine, when it came, was completely black.

We stared at the tin in stupefied silence. What was this? What did it mean?

Eventually my father broke the silence.

'I have blackwater fever,' he said. His voice was calm and unemotional. The doctor in him was analysing the evidence and giving his diagnosis. 'I know what transfusions and medication I need, but we have nothing here. I am going to die.'

Those were the last words I ever heard from him. He may have spoken to Mum later but I did not hear his voice again. He lay down on the floor and we covered him to keep him warm. I felt useless, numbed by the enormity of the disaster that faced us. There was nothing I could do. Not a single thing. The future looked unimaginably hostile and dangerous. The great man who had inspired me, frightened me, taught me and loved me was down. There would never be anyone like him in my life again.

For three days he fought a losing battle. But oh how he fought! Even so, bit by bit, his hold on life loosened and on the third day he slipped into a coma. We tried to do the normal everyday things like collecting firewood and preparing a meal, but the desolation was overwhelming. Finally, towards evening, my father's distress grew and it was clear that the end was near. My mother hurriedly passed me a cooking pot with some rice in it and told me to go to the stream and wash the rice for dinner. I knew the meaning of that instruction and I was grateful for her thoughtfulness and tact.

The sun had slipped behind the Patkoi Hills but it still shone through the trees which lined the distant crests, bathing them in brilliant yellow that looked like gold dust. I sat by the bank, swilling the water over the rice, unable to think clearly about anything. So many confused emotions crowded in, but the one that dominated was an overpowering fear of the future without my father. It was a natural reaction but it diminished the instinct for survival. A single-minded determination to reach our journey's end was the only thing that would get us through.

What happened next only confirmed that a wounded animal is quickly set upon. It began, as such sinister occurrences usually do, in a perfectly normal way, when I realised that someone was crossing the stream towards me. Still dazed, I took no notice until something snapped in my mind: a dark shadow had flitted across the water. I looked up to find a Chinese soldier standing near me. Bits of torn uniform hung from his scrawny frame, barely covering the dirty bandage that was wrapped around a wound in his thigh. His black sunken eyes stared at me from a gaunt face, which was made more menacing by the rag tied around his shaven head.

He waved a bundle of currency notes at me and indicated he would exchange it for the rice. I shook my head. He persisted. I refused. Realising that I was too far from the longhouse to summon help, he grew bolder and stepped forward. Evidently the scoundrel was going to take the rice from me! I could not believe it. My father, who I had thought was immortal, was dying, yet there was no time for private grief before foul reality burst in. What did this fellow expect me to do? Run? Give him the rice? Plead for mercy?

'Bullshit!' I screamed. 'Come on, you bastard.'

Without warning my pent-up feelings exploded in an avalanche of raw energy. Totally out of control, I stood up and bawled the most foul, most blood-curdling abuse straight into the soldier's face. I felt not the slightest fear or hesitation as I prepared myself for violence. The whole lot: this hell hole, my dying father, my sick family, the barbaric Chinese, bloody Japs, useless British, faithless God, Clive North, everything, blew my mind apart. This was the last straw. I wasn't going to take any more – I would dish it out instead. An eye for an eye: this was the law of the jungle, clean, swift and free from debilitating compromises.

I felt the power of my rage as I turned on the fellow with a rock in my right hand. I was only just 12 years old, but I was prepared to fight him to the end. I heard myself howling like an animal as we swung blows at each other. My black hatred for the Chinese who had robbed and humiliated us burst out. The fellow stood his ground for ten seconds. Then, like the coward that he was, he fled across the stream towards the Chinese army huts. Still my rage consumed me. Even though he was moving away, I went on screaming abuse at him until I was exhausted.

That man would never know how close he came to death – either his or mine. He was going to take the only food we had; the precious rice that Mum had entrusted to me. There was no way I could allow him to do that: I'd owed it to my family to fight.

I could hardly breathe as the reaction to the confrontation set in. Then without warning the dam broke. My spiritual and mental resilience crumbled and I sobbed – just like a 'big girl' as Georgie would have said – 'Father, don't go! Don't leave us in this hell! Don't go, Father. Hold on. Don't go!'

There was no stiff upper lip, no 'men don't cry', no 'Steady the Buffs' and no pride. None of those things mattered. Only the four people in that longhouse mattered. Without them I was nothing. Without my father we were doomed. Where was his God, the one he walked with and talked with? The one who said, 'Whatsoever ye shall ask in my name, that will I do.' If ever there was a time to reach down from heaven and help him, it was now.

Time passed and the shadows of the night stole across the valley, erasing the outlines of the hills and the forest so stealthily that the stars had replaced them before I became conscious that I was alone in the dark. A strange effect of the night was the way sounds carried, for the ripple of the stream beside me was transformed into the clear bell-like notes of a musical instrument. Even the baritone clearing his throat by the trees was only a barking deer calling his friends. And then there were the lights, dancing in the canopy of the jungle away to my left. Were they fireflies? Or were they the nats my mother knew, spirits from the natural world of earth, air, fire and water? Facing the jungle, I held my palms together in homage, for where else could I turn?

I went on sitting by the stream, utterly washed-out and cold. I have no idea how long I waited. Then I heard my mother's plaintive cry echoing in the wind and I knew it was over. I had heard that cry once before, was it a century ago? Now the same voice seared the mind again with its lament.

'William ... William ... William ...'

I had seen her grief when Richard was killed, her white face streaked with tears, dust in her long black hair as she crouched on the floor like a wounded animal. I knew she would be like that in the longhouse now. I should have gone to her, but I wanted to hide somewhere warm and safe until this nightmare was over and we were all together again. But this was reality and there was no escape. Thousands in the Hukawng Valley had faced this moment of truth, alone and in their own way. There could be no exceptions. It had to be faced. My father was dead.

Eventually Maisie called me back to the longhouse. It was dark inside and it took a few seconds for my eyes to adjust, but when they did I noticed that in the place where my father slept was a shape wrapped in a blanket.

I felt very cold, colder than I had ever felt before as I huddled with the others on the floor, staring at this shape. Everyone was crying except me – not because I did not feel sorrow but because fear had gripped me like a gigantic vice. My hands and shoulders shook with it while my mind seemed on the verge of coming apart. If a man as strong and dominant as my father could be struck down in three days, then weaklings like Mum, Maisie, George and me stood no chance of getting to India. One by one, we too would be wrapped in a blanket and thrown into the jungle. Worse still, who would be the last one to go, and would that person be as insane as the poor Indian woman? Would it be me?

# 15  *The Man Is Born*

Our only comfort during that careworn night was the certain knowledge that it would pass and daylight would return. Even so, the leaden hours dragged by. We clung to each other for comfort but there was very little sleep for anyone. At last the pale light of a new day lit the forest tree-tops, signalling that the time had come for us to perform the final act of yesterday's drama.

I had avoided thinking about the practical consequences of my father's death, but as the minutes passed the reality that we would be without him for the rest of my life began to gnaw at me again. My mind began to play tricks, for although a small part of it acknowledged that the figure on the floor was my father, the rest assured me that his death was a mistake and that he was about to sit up and ask for a cup of tea. I kept on pestering my poor long-suffering mother to check the body, in case my father had woken from a deep sleep which she had mistaken for a coma. Eventually, when she could bear it no longer, she turned the blanket back and told George and me to come forward and kiss Father goodbye.

His face was still and calm, almost angelic. The deep frown that he had worn as he struggled for his life had vanished, and his expression was peaceful and untroubled. When I bent and kissed his forehead it was cold and unyielding.

'Goodbye, Father', I whispered, half expecting a reply.

Only then did I accept that my father was dead. Only then did I weep openly for the strong man who had fallen.


Meanwhile Maisie had sent a message to North telling him of my father's death and asking him to make arrangements for the burial. Since we knew from past experience that we were likely to have a long wait, we ate a little rice and went about our daily chores, subdued but calm. I am sure the others saw the future with a pessimism too deep for my childish understanding. As for me, I felt light-headed and bewildered.

Some time in the afternoon when George and Maisie were asleep, my mother began to describe to me the problems that lay ahead of us. There was some talk of the tough climb over the Patkoi Hills, which I knew about already. But then my mother told me bluntly that life in a strange country without money, papers or the protection of my father was going to be immensely difficult. This was startling news. I had assumed that after this hideous trek, we would enter a land where peace and harmony would enable us to build Camelot again. However, I was even less prepared for her next remark.

'Stevie, you are the last Brookes. Daddy is dead and Maisie and Georgie are very sick and may not live. We depend on you now. You must always do your best. And never forget your family.'

Though I did not realise it then, my mother's words loosened my last hold on childhood. From then on I became to all intents and purposes the incarnation of my father, Major Brookes, driving myself remorselessly in every situation to prove that I was worthy of his name. Like some solitary Praetorian guard, abandoned when the legions sailed away, I went on defending my hilltop standard, screaming war cries and waving my rusting sword at the world until, decades later, I realised it was all for nothing. Yet I know my mother acted with love and the best of intentions. I touch her feet in tribute to an outstanding survivor.

In the longhouse at Shingbwiyang we waited all day by Father's body. We were far from confident as the hours passed, for all too often we had seen the consequences of relying on others to deal with burials. But there was no other option, for we were too weak to take care of it ourselves.

By early evening it seemed probable we would have to spend another night beside my father's body. Our greatest worry was the hideous prospect of what would happen if the burial was delayed for yet another day. So we were unmistakably relieved when two British soldiers, Major Leane and Sergeant Shaw, accompanied by a couple of Kachins, arrived in our corner of the longhouse while we were preparing our evening meal.

Major Leane had shown genuine concern for us in the last stages of Father's illness, visiting us with a few medicines and a special treat of fresh meat to cook. We were enormously grateful to him for all the help he had given us. And now here he was again in our moment of despair, offering Mum his condolences and comforting her with kind words.

With unusual care, the Kachins placed Father in their makeshift stretcher made from a blanket slung between two poles. As they lifted it onto their shoulders, Major Leane and Sergeant Shaw stood to attention and saluted. That moment is etched for ever on my mind, for even then I knew that by that single act they had healed the wounds of recent weeks. My father was a warrior and he had been treated as such. I knew he would have chuckled and said to me, 'That's how we do it it in the army, son.' I thank Major Leane and Sergeant Shaw for their honourable conduct all those years ago.

As Father was carried away, Mum and Maisie began to sing the hymn 'God be with you till we meet again'. George and I joined in, but after a few bars I could not go on. The storm inside me was too fierce. It should never have happened to Father like this, after a lifetime of service to God, King and Country.

And so in a corner of the forest close to Shingbwiyang where the wild orchids bloom and the sambur tread with care at sundown, he was laid to rest. The noble hunter, the shikari, was home at last.

Maisie went to see North to get a death certificate and she records that he would not give her anything special for Mum. But Major Leane came to see us and comfort us again. He brought Mum a mosquito net, thus increasing our chances of avoiding malaria by about ninety per cent. He also arranged for a young man called Reggie Fenton, who belonged to the same detachment of the Burma Auxiliary Force as Richard and Willie, to transfer from his hut to our longhouse so that we had a grown man to fend for us.

It was a remarkable coincidence that Reggie was in Shingbwiyang with us, for his family had lived directly opposite ours in Maymyo and we had been friends for many years. He was about Maisie's age and his youngest brother Noel had been my contemporary at school. I had uneasy memories of the Fenton family, for one day before the war, as I came back from school, I saw my father riding out of Lindfield on his bicycle with his shotgun in his hand. I just had time to dive behind a bush before he opened fire, shooting the Fentons' dog Blackie stone dead. Then he cycled back to Lindfield with his shotgun still reeking, like Wyatt Earp or Doc Holliday galloping into Tombstone after a shoot-out.

At home I discovered that the Fentons' dog had bitten Maisie, an offence so heinous in my father's eyes that he rode out, posse fashion, and potted Blackie. In fact the dog-bites and the awful anti-rabies injections that followed so traumatised my sister that she suffered from nerves for the rest of her life. As for the Fentons, they hid in their house for several days until my unpredictable father had cooled down.

At last in early August, with heavy rain still pounding down and storms howling through the valley, we were told to move out of our disintegrating charnel house into some new huts built on higher ground. Another fortnight and there would have been no survivors left to move. Even so, it was obvious that many of those struggling along the narrow path that led to the new quarters would be too weak to continue the trek to India. Incarceration in this insanitary place, without proper food or medical support, had drained our physical strength and weakened our resolve. All concentration camps have that effect. Yet a few months earlier, of our own free will, we had all made our way through the worst part of the Hukawng Valley to reach Shingbwiyang. We were highly motivated then, stronger and ready to take our chances with the Patkoi Hills and the weather. But the authorities had prevented us from going on and turned us into weaklings.

At first sight the new huts, which were towards North's bungalow, looked a distinct improvement on the ones we had left. A small area of jungle had been cleared and within this glade were about a dozen bamboo huts, each large enough to take two or three families. Entry was via the familiar stepped tree-trunk but the roof was made from a single sheet of tarpaulin instead of the insect-laden local thatch.

Our hut provided shelter for two groups of people. The first, consisting of our family and Reggie, lay against one wall like five very pale sardines. The second, against the far wall, consisted of the Anglo-Indian with the infected leg, plus the Indian lady and her little son.

Within a couple of days of moving in, Maisie was showing all the symptoms of cerebral malaria – a terminal illness in our present circumstances. Her fever and ague were now accompanied by severe headaches. Soon her mind began to wander and she became delirious. Georgie, who now looked like a skeleton, went down with dysentery – another fatal illness in the jungle – and began to fade as rapidly as Maisie.

Mum was still fighting to save her children but I could tell she was close to cracking. She became more and more tense and agitated with worry and fatigue. But every day she patiently fed them her miracle cure: water from boiled rice for George and 'pish–pash' for Maisie, which was the same water with a spoonful of boiled rice in it. Then she would tend to them as if they were at home at Lindfield on soft beds, instead of on hessian sacks in a bamboo hut. Providentially I remained well, despite the shared confinement. I had developed an adult strength and tenacity. In my head now I was a man, with no more fear of the jungle and no doubt that I would survive.

However I kept Maisie's diary going for the next ten days, and my childish scrawl is a vivid reminder that I was still a child, though called on to face a man's challenges. The first was to get medical help to Maisie. My record states that a Dr Bell came and gave Maisie an injection, though I cannot remember how I got him there. It seems that I also wrote asking him to come and see her again. What he made of my scrawl I do not know, but he came and gave medicine to both George and Maisie. At last, their infections were being properly treated on a regular basis.

Meanwhile rations had to be picked up from North's compound, the jungle scoured for food and the lot made into edible dishes. Mum and I shared the cooking and produced such delights as rice with bully beef and fresh bamboo shoots, chapattis with wild yam curry and 'green something', and an occasional roasted fish when I was lucky.

There was food in the jungle if you knew how to go about it. I dug yams from the banks of streams and cut bamboo shoots from the base of the huge clumps, which were usually infested with snakes. Yams were like potatoes but slippery, while bamboo shoots were delightfully crunchy when boiled. I have no idea what the botanical name for 'green something' was, but my mother showed me the right things and I did the collecting. The leaves were like spinach and the stalks like asparagus.

Sometimes I was able to haggle with the Nagas for a few handfuls of glutinous local rice, which was bluish-black. We cooked this in traditional jungle style by stuffing a piece of green bamboo stalk, about a foot long and just over an inch in diameter, with wet raw rice. The open end was plugged with twisted leaves and the tube thrust into hot embers for about twenty minutes. When the charred tube was removed and the walls were peeled back, it left a rod of deliciously steamed rice held together by the paper-like inner lining of the bamboo tube. The aroma and taste were exquisite.

I caught fish with a bent pin – truly – and we tried making the small ones into fermented fish paste – a revolting culinary mistake that was never repeated. Later on a Naga hunter showed me how to fish with my Gurkha kukri. I crouched in the middle of the stream with the hilt in my right hand an inch above the surface of the water and parallel to it. I then pulled the tip of the blade back with my left hand against the downward pressure of my right.

When I opened my left hand the blade swished down with amazing speed, cleaving through the water and slicing into a stationary catfish.

To complement these victuals I 'invented' bread by putting some well-kneaded dough made of 'atta' (coarse brown flour) into an old bully-beef tin, and leaving it over-night near the hearth. The warmth and the natural yeast in the coarse flour, or perhaps the bugs in the air, fermented the dough. Next morning I pushed the tin into some hot embers and hey presto – bread. I say without the slightest doubt or humility that no one apart from me produced fresh bread in Shingbwiyang!

About a mile beyond Shingbwiyang I came across a deserted smallholding. A pile of rotting thatch was all that remained of a Kachin hut, but here and there a cultivated plant struggled to hold its own against the encroaching jungle. I recognised two climbing plants which grew at Lindfield, and from each hung one solitary fruit. The first was a type of gourd called *Gurkha thi-kwa-thee* in Burmese, which was delicious fried in batter. The other was a 'bitter gourd' which was an acquired taste but which Mum said was 'good for you', whatever that meant. I also found a sickly tapioca tree but the roots were not worth keeping. A luckier find was a banana tree, which although devoid of fruit provided me with three large leaves which Mum cut up into 'plates'. A piece of stem was cut out as well because the inner core was edible.

On one of my forays into the jungle I also discovered two wild lime trees flush with fruit. Although the limes were yellow they were very sour. Ignoring this, however, I climbed up and collected enough limes to share with the camp members. It was while distributing them that I made an extraordinary discovery.

Calling at a hut nearby I was dumbfounded when a lady appeared at the door who looked exactly like Miss Doyle, my teacher from the boys' school in Maymyo.

'Oh, hello. You're Stephen Brookes, aren't you?' she said.

I panicked. Was it really possible to meet my teacher in the middle of the Hukawng Valley? What a strange world this was! If it was Miss Doyle, she had caned me several times the previous year for minor offences such as forgetting my thirteen-times tables, so my conditioned reflex was to run. But I hesitated long enough to reply politely: 'Good afternoon, Sir. I have brought you some limes' – regardless of sex, all teachers were called 'Sir' at our school. Don't ask me why.

Sir looked down at this ragged urchin and said, rather whimsically: 'I see.'

At that point my nerve gave out. I dumped the limes and ran. 'Bloody hell!' I thought. 'The old bat might have given me some homework or caned me for picking sour limes.'

Back at our hut I realised that my father's silver penknife, which was engraved with his name, had fallen out of my pocket while I was climbing the lime trees. Though I searched through the grass and jungle beneath them many times, I never found the penknife, and the loss of this keepsake filled me with remorse.


To add to our problems, we now began to be disturbed at night. First the bamboo floor started bending and creaking as if someone was moving stealthily in the inky blackness.

*The Man Is Born*

Then one night the mosquito net began to move and we heard laboured breathing. George yelped as a hand grabbed his leg and even as I moved my legs back, a hand brushed my feet. It was terrifying. We had no torches, no light whatever. What the devil was going on? I let out a yell and Maisie followed in her delirium.

Reggie hurriedly lit a match – and there was the crazy Indian lady crawling about on the bamboo floor. Mum shouted at her to go away and she was back in her corner before the match burnt out. But during the next two months we were treated several times to alarming nocturnal wanderings, heavy breathing and ghost-like hands in the night. We never found out why the poor woman wandered in the dark, but Mum believed she may have been looking for her lost family.

Even in the new huts refugees were still dying. Their agonies seemed to be worst at night, like the crazed wanderings of the Indian lady. One night Mum, Reggie and I were chatting by the light of a candle which Reggie had managed to lay hands on, when a commotion broke out in one of the huts. Someone began to thrash about in the undergrowth and a woman's voice screamed what sounded like 'Brian' or 'Bell'.

Almost immediately there was the sound of running feet and the awful laboured breathing of someone gasping for air. I knew that sound. My father had fought for his life like this. Terrified that the light would attract the man into our hut, I put my bare hand over the candle flame, plunging us into darkness. The woman's cries and the loud gasping continued for some time, then all was quiet. Next morning the man lay dead in the undergrowth barely a few yards from our door.

A couple of weeks later two strong young men in a hut near us went down with dysentery, going from normality to total prostration in about two days. Towards the end they lay on the floor at the entrance to their hut, shouting to people by name, over and over again, to come and help them. But no one came. Finally when Mum could stand it no more, she put some food in a banana leaf and told me to take it to them.

When I saw them lying there, sunken-eyed and filthy, I was scared to go too close in case I caught some terrible sickness. But when they beckoned me I knew I had to do it. I took a deep breath, ran into their hut, left the food on the floor and ran back home before I breathed again. During the night we heard their tearful call: 'Thank you, Mrs Brookes. Thank you, Mrs Brookes,' repeated several times. Then all was quiet. It frightened me that even the strongest among us could be struck down so decisively. Clearly the new huts did not necessarily bring immunity from tropical diseases.

I can still hear the voices, see the faces and know precisely the location of all the huts, including that of the two young men. I see our hearth with Mum squatting beside it, George lying on some sacking beside her, then Maisie rambling in delirium, my little sleeping place next to her, and Reggie's spot with his .303 rifle beside it. How fascinating to remember. How peaceful to forget.

Maisie, in her delirium, chatted happily to her fiancé Frank and to Father, members of our family, and friends.

'Fra ... Frank ... ise ... ise ... vry ... sik ... oooh ... Jan ... Janet ... plees ... see ... sik ... no ... hullo ... Frank ... mmmm ... Dadee ... aaah.'

It was very scary, particularly the night-time hallucinations, which reminded me of the death of the Anglo-Indian gentleman. Occasionally I said 'Shut up, Boozie,' but Mum was cross with me for my intolerance.

By the end of August there were definite signs of improvement and although Maisie and George were both still very weak it seemed that the worst had passed. We now had fairly intelligent conversations and an occasional joke, but more important, they could sit up and take stock of their surroundings. The keeping of the diary had also reverted to Maisie, so events were recorded for posterity in her pristine handwriting instead of my spidery squiggles.

One of the first entries made when she became reasonably compos mentis was: '21 August. North paid us a visit.'

It was his first and only visit to us while we were stuck in Shingbwiyang from June to October 1942. I have no idea what was said nor did I care. Another entry notes that a few days later Major Leane and Sergeant Shaw came to see us. They undertook to despatch letters to Maisie's fiancé Frank and to Dennis, my eldest sister's husband, presuming they were still alive somewhere in India.

Now it was Mum I really began to worry about. Her children were almost out of danger, but she had paid the price in strength and energy. She was thin, her long black hair now streaked with white and her face lined with worry. What a mockery if she were to die so that her children could live. As the fittest in the family I did my best to help by making sure that rations, medicines and jungle vegetables were always available, so that she had only to take care of the other two. Reggie also helped with collecting rations, chopping firewood and carrying water from the stream in the valley.

While I was fishing for supper one day, I was distracted by the amazing sight of a parachutist drifting down from a strange plane circling high above Shingbwiyang. I ran down the trail to the meadow by our old longhouses, but by the time I arrived the excitement was over. I was told that a doctor and two Indian assistants had landed. I was torn between crying with relief and spitting with disgust, for they were four months too late. There was only a handful of survivors left to tend. Yet over 40,000 evacuees, plus the remnants of the Chinese Fifth Army, had arrived in this accursed place.

We were still treated to the occasional burst of rain, but the ground was drying out as summer turned to autumn. One fine afternoon in late September, I persuaded Mum to come with me on a conducted tour of what had been my turf during the darkest weeks of our lives. This stretch of jungle was like the centre of a town to me, where game trails criss-crossed the track like side-streets off a main road. Some trails led to water, or to fruit trees or open grassland, just as the side-streets led to shops, offices and parks. Until now I had led a solitary existence in this rural town, concerned only with finding food for my family. But as the pressure for survival eased I longed to share my attraction, and indeed affection, for this secluded world with Mum.

So, her hand in mine, I led her along the jungle game-trails, pointing out the trees, flowers and views of special interest as one would a theatre, bridge or street in town. I showed her where I fished and where the yams and the lime trees grew; we tip-toed down the hidden track which led to the Naga village and gazed wistfully at the branches of bright orchids. But when we got to the clumps of bamboo where I used to search for shoots, a huge black snake unwound itself from the base.

Mum turned tail with a querulous squeak and refused to come back, though I assured her I was an accomplished snake-killer. I suppose the urban equivalent would be coming up against a mugger. At any rate that was the end of the tour, for she would not be drawn into the jungle again. However, despite the surprise ending, I remember that afternoon with a lasting sense of pleasure and peace.

On a fine day, Mum usually seated Maisie and George in the sun by the stairs, where they washed themselves in a leisurely way with a bamboo tube of water which Reggie fetched from the stream. Georgie was very weak and so thin that each rib and joint stood out sharply from his greyish flesh. Against all the odds, my hero was still alive, though stronger men had perished. There was always some banter between us.

'Hey, Stevie,' he would call out. 'You're such a big coward. Reggie said you ran when a baby snake looked at you.'

'Nah. It was only a worm Georgie, so I cooked it for your dinner.'

My own private convenience was a spectacular affair. To reach it you had to climb over a huge tree trunk which had been partly blown over an escarpment. The heavy root section lay embedded in the soft earth on the crest, but the rest of the tree was in space. I shuffled along the trunk until I reached the far end, where I would squat down, steady myself by holding on to the smaller branches, and dream.

Thirty feet below me were the tops of trees, which gradually faded into the rolling plains of the Hukawng away to my right. No amount of money could buy anywhere as breathtaking as my secret place in the sky.

Since no one had the nerve to follow me along the tree-trunk, I enjoyed complete privacy except for the red ants which converged on me if I lingered too long. Poor Mum always screamed at me when I set off because she was convinced I would fall asleep or dream and drop off into the jungle far below. Sometimes she would stand on firm ground and shout, 'Steeee, Steeee, Steeee,' until I gave up and shuffled back home.

September passed and all our hopes of rescue faded. The Dakotas still flew over the Patkoi Hills but there was no longer any joy for me in looking at them. Too much grief, too many mountains, separated us. There were rumours every day that we were leaving but nothing came of them. There were now only two months left to Christmas. It would soon be 1943. There was a distinct coolness in the air at night and even the jungle seemed less oppressive as the sunshine filtered through the canopy, painting the forest floor with light.

So much time had passed. Though I stood a good chance of reaching India if we started now, the others were in no fit state to climb the Patkoi Hills. I walked down to my favourite spot by the creek with a heavy heart. I missed my Old Man, his strength and confidence; but most of all I missed hearing his voice.

'Father,' I whispered. 'If your spirit lives here by the trees and the water, hear me. Hold my hands and give me strength.'

When the sun dipped behind the distant mountain ridges, I made my way home along a winding game-trail where the imprint of my bare feet in the soft earth blended with the delicate spoors of jungle animals. A few minutes later I saw the fires from the huts glowing warm orange through the split bamboo walls, so reminiscent of the autumn 'Full Moon of Tazaungmon' that once shone on my lost home, Lindfield. Did fire-balloons still sail through the night sky of Japanese-occupied Burma during the Full Moon festival, carrying prayers and offerings to the nats in heaven? Or had the pragmatic Burmese decided that an automatic rifle was more realistic?

As I approached our settlement the unusual sound of laughter seemed to drift in the wind. Real laughter was rare these days. Could it be the normal sort I wondered, or was it another case of someone floating in the happy land of delirium? Before I reached our hut the answer was clear: it was definitely the normal sort. Then more laughter and the excited chatter of our neighbours as I drew near. I ran up the log stairs and found our household more animated than I had seen them for months. Together they whooped, 'We're leaving! We're leaving Shingbwiyang.' The rest was drowned in giggles, more laughter – and tears.

Why was I crying? For a moment the knowledge of freedom was so painful and confusing I could do nothing but weep. Then the log-jam of sorrow and anger was swept away, leaving me gasping with joy and thankfulness. As I wiped my tears and laughed with my family it felt as if heavy chains had fallen from my back.

I held my mother's thin hands and felt their warmth. I said to her, '*Amaye, ben-neh-lay-ther?*' Mother, how are you?

She smiled and nodded. I left it at that, for I guessed that her mind was filled with dark memories of the past and fears of the future.

'We're off in two days,' said Maisie.

I wondered if my Old Man had heard my prayer. It would not have surprised me, for my father could always sort out the things that God messed up.

That night I sat at our doorway while the others slept. I should have been ecstatic yet I felt beaten. This decision had been so long in coming that I hardly felt it mattered what happened next, for Father and Willie and countless others would not be leaving with us. But one thing I knew: Shingbwiyang had marked each one of us so deeply that it would for ever be a source of private grief.

# 16  *I Have a Dream*

It was 1 October 1942: something was definitely afoot in North's compound when I strolled down there to enjoy the gossip. The padlocked godown, which looked like a redoubt in *The Last of the Mohicans,* was wide open and soldiers were busy stacking bags of rice and flour against the outer bamboo railing. Even more curious, under the trees near the main gate a group of Naga porters were sorting through their carrying gear. These stocky fellows, with their bulky calves and splayed-out feet, could carry huge loads on their backs with these harnesses. The design was ingenious because the load was distributed across the neck, shoulders and back by cords which passed through a wooden yolk on the shoulders and ended in a broad strap across the forehead.

But, clever though the harnesses were, I was more impressed by the Nagas' magnificent dahs of sharp steel. These swords, which were about two feet long, had elegant handles of carved teak or horn from which hung tufts of animal hair. For an additional touch of glamour, the dahs were carried in wooden scabbards bound with strands of cane woven into intricate patterns. They were the jungle man's equivalent of the scout-knife but far more sophisticated, for with a dah you could catch fish, build a hut, cut down trees, pare your nails, chop up a chicken, slice greens, build a canoe and fight a war. In the days before the British brought their boring law and order into the wild hills and valleys, these dahs were the Naga headhunters' answer to the guillotine. No wonder the adult males wore them draped across their backs in a loop of cane, with all the aplomb of a Captain of the Coldstream Guards.

I longed to own a dah, but there were problems. A few weeks before I had innocently tried to buy one from a hunter I met in the jungle but he reacted with such hostility that I feared for my life. When I mentioned this to Reggie he told me that my suggestion was equivalent to making an offer for the man's wife, though how he arrived at this conclusion I do not know.

Later that afternoon, the news of our departure was confirmed by a sane person – that is, a person not suffering from a nervous disorder or a terminal illness. I mean no disrespect to my fellow refugees, but so many people were by now non-compos mentis that even the most mundane conversation could quite suddenly turn into a farce.

There was the half-naked reincarnation of Mahatma Gandhi who always began his conversation with the words 'Now look here, General ...' – even when he was talking to me. I took exception to this as I believed I was really that legendary white man Rajah Brooke of Sarawak, supreme ruler of the Sea Dayaks of Borneo. Another kept insisting:

'It's true, my sister sent me a letter yesterday.' We had so many screws loose between us that we almost rattled. However there could be no doubt that this latest information was authentic because it came directly from North's compound: we were free to leave tomorrow.

In our corner of the woods the euphoria sparked off by this news quickly evaporated, for Mum was slipping rapidly into a physical and emotional breakdown. She had borne the break-up of her family and her own transition from riches to rags with characteristic Asian stoicism. Yet in spite of her outward calm, I knew she was shaken to the core by Father's death. Caring for Maisie and Georgie had temporarily taken her mind off her loss, but three months later, that and the knowledge that she was about to leave her native country must have preyed on her mind.

Late in the afternoon, when she was moving some pieces of bamboo near the fireplace, a split section slipped and slashed her wrist. Instantly her clothes, the wall and floor were splashed by a stream of blood. It happened so quickly that for a few seconds we were transfixed with shock. Then there was pandemonium as we tumbled over each other in our efforts to grab her arm and stop the bleeding. Cooking vessels clattered about in the hearth as she writhed on the bamboo floor, struggling with us, screaming and shivering as though possessed.

I had never seen her like this before. She looked so wild that I was scared to get too close in case she turned on me, but the others managed to calm her by degrees. Strips of cloth hastily torn from a shirt were used to bandage her wrist and bring the bleeding under control. Several minutes later she had relaxed and was breathing easily. Gradually sanity returned. Before long we had Mum resting peacefully under a blanket while we cleaned up around her and washed the blood off ourselves.

Those few minutes of frenzy when my mother finally snapped left a lasting impression on me. The sight of her blood dripping down the wall, her torment, her utter misery – it was too much. I had to go and sit in the rainforest for an hour because I was shaking so much.

'Please, please, Mother, never again.' I whispered.

Walking thoughtfully back along the trail I knew so well, I said farewell to the jungle with the same feeling of loss as on that bleak day in April when we took our leave of Lindfield and Maymyo. For this had been my kingdom since Father died, my one square mile of wild rainforest through which I moved like the shadow of a deer. My rage against the unforgiving Valley of Death was tempered by the knowledge that it had tamed me. But more, it had educated me, both physically and spiritually, in a university without equal.

In the beginning I had lashed out in fear and anger, fighting the monsoon and the jungle with the panic of a drowning child. Gradually I had learned to swim, to coexist with the elements and the jungle rather than trying to remain separate from them. And I was generously rewarded in a way I did not understand until many years later.

But now it was time for me to take my leave of this mystical valley. A last affectionate glance at the stream where the Naga had taught me how to catch fish with a dah, then down the trail to the longhouses, past the glade with the lime trees, through the field of 'green something' and finally to the little knoll where the bamboo clumps and wild ginger grew. High above me, the canopy of branches was silhouetted against the grey sky; higher still a pair of kites circled lazily in a current of warm air; and at my feet were the scratch-marks and footprints of deer. The forest was silent, yet full of life. As I traced the outline of the footprints with the tips of my fingers I was enthralled and humbled. 'Yes, I know. I know now,' I thought. On the spur of the moment, I held my palms together in homage to the wonder of this life. Then it was time to face the problems of a different reality.

Mum was asleep by the fireplace and breathing deeply. I gazed at the thin figure, still dressed in a stained blouse and longyi, and was amazed at how fragile she had become. Her eyes were buried deep in their boney sockets while her hair, once beautiful with jewels and flowers, tumbled uncombed on the bamboo floor. The blood-stained bandage was still wrapped around her wrist. Here was someone who had reached the limit of her endurance. She could give no more.

I have often wondered how the accident really happened. She knew as well as the rest of us that the edge of a split bamboo was as sharp as a razor-blade and had to be treated with the greatest care. Perhaps it was just tiredness and a moment of carelessness that had caused the accident.

Or was it something more disturbing? Mum's suffering over the past twelve months must have been more terrible than any of us could even imagine. Had her tremendous courage forsaken her for an instant? We shall never know.

The sun set and darkness fell on our last night in Shingbwiyang. So it was true that all things pass. How

thoughtless I had been as I stood on the back seat of the
Baptist Church in Maymyo, grinning as I looked out over
my family's heads while they sang:

> Time, like an ever-rolling stream,
> Bears all its sons away;
> They fly forgotten, as a dream
> Dies at the opening day.

I could not sleep for the memories. Everything had gone:
Lindfield and everything in it; my people scattered before I
was old enough to know them.

I saw the marching columns of troops, Willie and
Richard and Father, moving through the swirling dust; the
men in my family, all eight of them, in crisp uniforms and
shining buttons. By heck! I was proud of them. I still had
my pride, even though I was in a bamboo hut in the middle
of a jungle and looking like a savage.

Tomorrow we would set out to walk another 128 miles
over the mountains to India. What then?

'We depend on you now.' That is what Mum had said.
'You are the last Brookes.'

Well, I knew my duty. As the Major would have said: 'No
excuses, son, just get on with it.'

There was excitement in the air as the occupants of our
hut awoke next day. After a quick breakfast of plain tea followed by left-over curry and rice we began the important
business of kitting ourselves up for this last journey. The
tally of my possessions was: one torn shirt, a pair of shorts

and my precious kukri – nothing else. So all I had to do was tuck my kukri into the string that served as a belt and I was ready to go.

The others were ready in a few minutes – apart from Mum and Georgie. They could be dressed, but that was all, for neither of them could walk. We had avoided facing this grim truth the previous day, hoping that somehow it would disappear in the morning. But we should have learnt from this journey that all situations move inexorably to their logical conclusion, and however painful that is it cannot be wished away.

Fortunately one of the compound staff had checked on the mobility of all the refugees and had made appropriate plans. We were given an assurance that Mum and Georgie would be carried by Naga porters. The refugees were to leave in two groups. Those who were fit enough to walk at a reasonable pace, without assistance, would set off first. Then would come a second group made up of the sick and infirm, who would be accompanied by porters and carriers. The two groups would camp together each night, and food and shelter would be provided. We were also told that Refugee Liaison Officers from the Indian Tea Association and their staff would help us along the route.

Since most people had been confined in germ-infested huts for five months, however, their ability to walk twelve miles, let alone 128 miles over the Patkoi Hills, was doubtful. So with alarm bells ringing in our heads, we settled Mum and Georgie comfortably on the floor of our hut to await their bearers and set out for the meadow.

'Hey, Stevie,' said my brave brother, as I stood in the doorway. 'Don't run off to India and leave us here.'

'As if I would, Georgie,' I replied gently. 'As if I would. I'll wait for you by the longhouse. I promise.'

I gave him a big wink and walked down the log stairs for the last time. They could be certain that, whatever happened, I would never leave them.

At midday the first trekkers set out on the track leading to India. Mum and George had joined us by this time. George was seated in a harness on the back of a Naga porter while Mum lay in a makeshift stretcher carried on the shoulders of two more. I winced when I saw them. Although my brother was only 14 he was much taller than the porter, so when he was lifted, his feet had dragged along the ground. The Naga, who was clearly a DIY expert, had solved this by bending George's knees back and tying his ankles to the seat. I knew he was in pain, but he always gave me a sunny smile and a wave when we passed one another. During the journey he never complained once, although I argued with his porter on at least three occasions for not releasing his ankles when they stopped for a rest. If I could award medals, I would proudly present one to George Seymour Brookes, the boy who fought the good fight with quiet determination and who never once asked the question which was on every other sufferer's lips: 'Why me?'

As for Mother, we could not see anything of her as she was entombed in the blanket which formed the base of the stretcher. But before we set out I heard her muffled call coming from its folds, much like the ghostly voice from the ancient Egyptian mummy which frightened the hell out of Boris Karloff: 'Steee, Maisie, stay together ... Don't get lost ... Stay together.'

With one voice we replied to Cleopatra, 'We're all right Mum. Relax. Don't worry.'

'Steee ... don't play in the jungle ... tigers ...'

We did not hear the rest because we quietly tiptoed away. Then my sister and I held hands, turned our backs on Shingbwiyang and started down the path that led to India.


'Free at last' I shrieked with joy. 'The sun has got his hat on ... Hip hip hip hooray ... The sun has got his hat on and he's coming out today ... Come on, catch me Boozie ... catch me ...'

Somehow the world looked different, brighter, more friendly. There was clean air to fill the lungs, refresh the mind; there was space and movement, and the rich smell of grass drying in the sun.

The first couple of miles were deceptively easy for they were on level ground. We walked hurriedly past the camp of the Chinese Fifth Army, once filled to bursting-point with hundreds of sick and hungry soldiers. Now it was difficult to see any signs of life. Several of the huts looked derelict, while around them all was the detritus of human living and the foul smell of death. Although we had been ambushed twice by Chinese soldiers and I had fought one of them, I could not help feeling sorry for these men, abandoned in a strange land far from home.

Beyond the Chinese camp was the river. Looking down on the easy flow of this placid stream, it was difficult to remember that only a month ago it had been a beast of immense power, devouring trespassers. Today we hopped across a few rocks, waded up to our knees for a few yards, and we were through.

Soon the thick jungle closed in around us, for we were in the Patkoi foothills. The familiar trudge along steep ridges followed by sharp descents and ascents began to tax our new-found muscles. As the day wore on the track became much steeper, the occasional glimpse of the horizon below us confirming that we were now several hundred feet high on the shoulder of a Patkoi ridge. The walking-sticks I had cut from a wayside clump of bamboo helped us to keep up a steady rhythm, but we knew that on this trek there was no rush. Unlike our private venture across the Valley of Death during the monsoon, this was an organised affair. Besides, it was sunny and dry, a rare experience after our long ordeal. The rainforest now had a kind of righteous beauty, a transformation due entirely to the absence of dead bodies. The monsoon rains had swept them away, concealing them discreetly under a mantle of mud. Strolling through this natural theatre filled with strange and wonderful things, I felt almost as if the show was a sort of matinee put on for our benefit. But I respected the jungle too much to be fooled, for I knew that in life, as in death, it was strictly neutral.

At five o'clock in the afternoon, by chance rather than clever steering, we reached a clearing in the jungle which looked strangely civilised. There were fires with real food bubbling in huge containers, shelter, laughter, even organised chaos. A voice called 'Hello Maisie.' We two had trekked eight miles that afternoon entirely on our own, so intent were we on enjoying our new freedom, and we had popped up in the right place at the right time. We sat on the grass drinking hot tea and giggling like a couple of schoolchildren who had climbed back into the dormitory without being spotted.

But although we had reached sanctuary, I was still full of fight. I strode through the fringe of jungle, slashing at bamboo clumps and slender treetrunks with my kukri. I had a peculiar feeling in my head, a kind of conditioned reflex from our own trek months ago, when it was my duty to cut firewood and bedding for the night. I went through these motions now, involuntarily. I knew it was strange, but I still chopped firewood, unable to resist the inner drive for survival. This routine was repeated at almost every camp we stopped at, a performance so puzzling that an officer spoke to my mother about it.

We waited another day at this camp since the second group with Mum, George and the porters had not arrived by nightfall. Perhaps it had dawned on the porters after the first hundred yards that carrying huge sacks of rice and incontinent refugees was not quite the easy job promised by the management.

At lunchtime on the second day, bored and bursting with energy, I persuaded Maisie to take a short stroll with me along the track. It was another beautiful day in the hills, with dappled sunshine rippling through the high canopy to light our path. After about half-an-hour we emerged from the forest and found ourselves on a grassy knoll on the edge of a high ridge.

The heavy silence gave the view a dream-like quality. Several hundred feet below us was the beginning of a vast plain which rolled along to where it melted into the sky over thirty miles away. We were so high that the tops of the trees merged with the mottled green of the plain, in which segments of winding rivers glinted in the sun like slivers of broken glass. Slightly to the right was an area of cleared land, dotted with brown shapes from which a blue haze drifted lazily in the afternoon breeze.

The tears were in my eyes before I could stop them, for I was looking down on Shingbwiyang and the immense sweep of the Hukawng Valley. We could not see its junction with the Kumon range, those mountains we had crossed with the Gurkhas in May, which lay more than 120 miles beyond the horizon. Five months of my life were laid out before me in this vast panorama. Standing on this hillside I had a moment of total recall and stark recognition of the lost past. The sense of desolation and loneliness was crushing.

I stood on the ridge while jumbled images flashed through my mind. Somewhere in the middle distance was the last sighting of Willie and the orphan girls, and down by the wood-smoke was my father. Now there was just Maisie and me. Yet I knew that if I lost control I would be in serious trouble, for the lesson of my mother's sudden breakdown and decline only three days earlier was not lost on me.

'Stevie, I'm scared. Let's go.'

I heard Maisie's voice but I could not respond. It was not only sorrow, it was anger at our impotence to influence the course of events. Bitterness against those who had stopped us at Shingbwiyang without adequate care. Rage at the armies of Japan, England and China, who had fought their private battles on another nation's land, careless of the consequences.

'Stevie. Don't stay here any longer. Come, let's go.' I realised that my sister was moving away.

It had been a profoundly disturbing experience. I can summon it up at will even as I sit here, though the bleak ghosts are not so active now.

We walked back to the camp to find that Mum and George and the rest of the people from the second group had all arrived safely. Another big tarpaulin was stretched between four tree-trunks to shelter them, and extra rice and bully beef was laid out on the banana leaf plates. There were so many good and cheerful things to talk about that the cheerless past was soon forgotten. Maisie and I never spoke about the view from the ridge again.

That night, while my stomach rumbled contentedly after a generous helping of hot food, I snuggled up close to my mother, wrapped my arms around her and drifted blissfully to sleep while she spun stories of the days when she and my father were young.

'... and then from Kalewa your Daddy went up the Chindwin river to Kindat to inspect the hospital ... He was the Senior Assistant Surgeon and we went together ... One night when the boat was not far from Kindat, we heard a tiger roaring in the jungle ... he always called from the same place and the serang said he was a man-tiger ... the tiger was looking for his longyi which was lost ... he was angry, because he could not become a man again until he had stepped back into his longyi three times ... Daddy wanted to hunt the tiger ... but the serang said the nats would be angry ...'

We covered thirty-two miles during the next four days, following a trail through the mountains that wound higher and higher until by the third day we reached a height of 4,000 feet. I remember that stretch as particularly gruelling since we had to climb for nine hours to reach the camp, which was sited twelve miles away. The porters were magnificent, but even they began to show signs of strain when they had to retrace their steps several times to pick up frail refugees who had collapsed by the wayside. I understood their irritation, for to them this mountain was a mere hillock which even their children could climb at a gallop.

I tried not to think about what Mum and George were going through for I had my own troubles. 'Stevie, I think I'm going to faint,' Maisie said suddenly.

'OK. I'll find a Naga to carry you.'

'Don't you dare, you little horror ...'

'Honestly. You'll enjoy it.'

'That's enough, you awful child. Come on, let's get going.'

'Look, there's a strong one. Hello Mr Naga Man. My sister's fainted.'

'Stop it. You dreadful, silly boy.'

And so we trotted off again, Maisie having made a spontaneous recovery at the mere idea of being slung across the back of a sweaty Naga warrior. I knew I was horrid but it did the trick.

We cleared the summit on the fourth day and began a pleasant descent to the village of Tagap Ga, where we halted for six days to allow the porters and their charges to recuperate and the organisers to plan. It was from now on that the Indian Tea Association and their staff played a vital role in our rescue. We owe them, their porters and road-builders a huge debt of gratitude. Without their help few of us would have survived the next hundred miles.

# 17 *Journey's End*

Of all the villages on this trek Tagap Ga was the prettiest. It stood on a wide grass-covered spur with pleasant views over rolling green hills and misty valleys. The huts and longhouses were dotted about at the end of the spur, giving the village a light and airy feel quite unlike the oppressive atmosphere of Shingbwiyang. Refugees had died here too in large numbers when they were trapped by the monsoon, but the hills seemed to give the place a sense of hope.

We left Tagap Ga reluctantly at midday on 14 October and enjoyed a pleasant trek of six miles before settling down for the night in a clearing beside a paddy field. The journey next day was another tough mountain climb that soon had us all groaning with fatigue. The distance to the next camp, on a river bank, was ten miles and we covered it in eight hours of solid marching. I remember wading across the river to the far bank where I lay down, closed my eyes and unwound in perfect peace, with the lulling sound of the river in the background. Then out of the blue I heard my mother's voice: 'Steee. Steee.'

Casually I turned my head to look at the people gathered along the bank, but Mum was not there. Perhaps it was someone else calling a friend. I settled down again and closed my eyes. Suddenly I heard it again, not through my ears but in my head: 'Steee. Steee.'

I sat up in alarm and shook Maisie, who was lying next to me.

'Can you hear Mum calling, Boozie?'

She listened for a few moments, shrugged her shoulders, then closed her eyes.

'Mum will be arriving with the second group soon,' she said. 'She'll be all right. Relax.'

As this seemed perfectly reasonable I lay down again for a few minutes but I could not settle. There was still a nagging feeling that I had overlooked a detail. Something was not in focus. With a start I realised that the second group was already here, and had been for some time.

I switched to full alert – head raised, tense, like a wild deer startled by the sound of a breaking twig. I knew, as clearly as though someone had spoken to me, that something had happened to Mum.

'Maisie, Maisie. Mum's in trouble. She's calling me.'

My sister looked confused. 'I can't hear anything,' she said. 'Honestly, I think you're imagining things, Stevie. Lie down.'

The next instant my mother called me again. It was a call full of fear, so powerful that it resonated in my head: 'Steee. Steee.'

Seconds later I was plunging through the river and racing up the far bank. The evening light was fading but there was no trace of fear in my heart. Charged up with anxiety and purpose, my kukri gripped firmly in my right hand, I sprinted back down the track for about a mile, certain that nothing could stop me. I still remember the strange primeval quality of the whole experience as I wove through the jungle like a savage, driven on by a fierce determination to reach my mother.

Then I saw her. She was huddled at the base of a large tree, looking down the track she knew I would use. I flung myself down and wrapped my arms round her in relief.

'My son. My son. I knew you would come. Everything's all right now,' she said in Burmese.

When I had calmed down, she told me that the exhausted porters had dumped her by the tree promising to send help when they reached the river. But as the light began to fade she realised they had simply abandoned her. So she called me.

Bemused, but relieved that I had responded to her call, I helped her to her feet while she steadied herself with a stick. Then we shuffled contentedly towards the river, reaching the campsite just in time for dinner.

This strange incident – coincidence, extra-sensory perception, thought transference, call it what you will – was my first experience of my sensitivity to distress in someone close to me. Over the last half century such 'contacts' have occurred several times. They can even wake me from sleep and distance does not seem to matter, whether it is from Australia, Burma, America or England. I have no explanation, scientific or otherwise, but the call is insistent and quite unlike the general feeling of anxiety about someone that we all experience.

Early next day, having warned the porters in sign-language not to dump my mother ever again, and they having responded by spitting at my feet and stroking their sharp dahs, I felt that honour had been satisfied on both sides and the matter could be discreetly dropped. Besides, I was never at my best fighting tribal wars before breakfast. My favourite time for spats was midday, when the opposition felt drowsy and I was awash with adrenalin.

We put in a sixteen-mile hike over the next two days. Showers slowed us down a bit and although they were nothing compared to the monsoon, it was uncomfortable walking in deep slush again.

We were still quite high up in the mountains and at night we would huddle round a blazing fire waiting for a meal. On one particular night, the Anglo-Indian man my father had saved by treating an open sore on his shin was sitting next to me. Further along a Naga was using our fire to cook his traditional meal of steamed blue rice in a bamboo tube thrust into the embers. Not being jungle-trained like me, the Anglo-Indian decided to stoke the fire. He threw a few logs on, raked the embers, picked up the charred tube of Naga dinner and flung it into the flames.

'What a bird-brain,' I thought.

The Naga, deprived of his dinner, went berserk. His dah was out and against the man's neck, while the man was flat on his back, squawking like a dying soprano. The Naga knelt on him, mouthing fearful threats that we all knew translated as: 'I'll split your tonsils, you snivelling excreta of a sow. You dare to incinerate my dinner! Prepare to die, you flea-ridden dog . . .'

I was thrilled at the idea of witnessing an authentic decapitation but the officials rushed in and spoilt my fun. The Naga was hauled off and the rescued man was dragged somewhere else. The man parted with money which the Naga tucked in his loincloth, there were a few grunts, and a sort of peace descended around our fire. After several minutes of relative calm, I emerged from behind my mother and hesitantly joined the queue for dinner.

A trek of eight miles next day brought us to the Tagaung Hka river which, to my relief, had a real bridge across it rather than the terrifying line of slippery logs and boulders we sometimes encountered. When we reached the far side, cries of joy rippled through our group for a rescue party from India, complete with more officers, porters and rations, was waiting for us. It was at this point I really began to feel that our escape from Burma might succeed. Of course this did not mean that all the people who left Shingbwiyang would survive. Indeed, several had already died and lay in graves beside the track. But we were close and there was a glimmer of hope.

Early next morning our group and the rescue party set off down the track, the unfamiliar sound of their chatter and laughter lifting my heart. I noticed that the refugees' appetite for news of any sort was insatiable, almost like a disease. Just for a moment I glimpsed Maisie talking to some officers, then she merged into the crowd and vanished. There was no sign of George either and I guessed Mum was holding court from her palanquin, her words muffled by her blanket as she was carried aloft.

For a while I wandered along on my own, realising with a pang of sadness that I was now a mere child once more, and therefore redundant. I was among healthy, civilised adults again and the talk was of journeys and distant destinations, of London and Australia, money and worries. There was no talk about where the best bamboo shoots grew or how to make bread in a bully-beef tin. But this was still my world, if only for a few more days, for around us was the realm of gibbons, butterflies, orchids and snakes where I was king. Without a second thought, I stepped off the track and melted into the jungle.

Moving quickly through the trees, I rejoined the track about half-a-mile ahead of the leading walkers. Now I was alone and I felt exhilarated. There was so much to see, to touch and to listen to that I felt like singing. Stepping lightly on the soft earth I moved noiselessly, always alert to the sudden movement of shadows, to the slightest unusual sound. I felt alive in every pore of my body.

A mile further on I came to a tiny brook of clear water flowing across the gravel bed: small silver fish darted about in swift clouds as they fed on the morsels of food drifting in the current. Higher up the brook I came across hundreds of tiny yellow butterflies spiralling upwards along a shaft of sunlight. They were enchanting, like sprites, and they remain a very special memory still. Undoubtedly it was a privilege for me to share these fleeting moments with them.

What happened next reminds me of my mother's dictum that too much happiness, too much laughter, only provokes the jealous gods to send down misfortune as a reprimand. It started when I noticed a piece of paper caught in some branches a few feet further up the brook. Instantly I sensed danger, for the presence of paper in virgin jungle was as unlikely as summer snow in the Hukawng. Moving cautiously, I slid into the brook and retrieved it – it was a ten rupee note.

'Something's not right, Stevie boy,' I said to myself.

My muscles tensed as I scanned the dark undergrowth around me, but nothing stirred. Then I glanced further upstream and saw more rupee notes, stacks of them, snagged on twigs, on rocks or washed into recesses in the bank.

Excited, I waded upstream gathering notes by the handful. I had never seen so much loose money lying around: it was a miracle. So intent was I on stuffing the rupees into my pockets that I ignored a familiar smell that grew stronger as I worked my way along the brook.

Suddenly a mass of blowflies swirled into the air with a resounding buzz. I spun round in alarm and saw it – a bloated corpse, limbs sprawled out, clothes strewn about, flies, maggots. It looked as though an animal had eaten part of it.

'Jesus Christ! Get out. Run,' was my only thought.

Gibbering with fright I plunged through branches and thorns, feeling no pain. Down the main track I sprinted, shrieking to keep away the nats, murderers, tigers and anything else that might be following me. I was so worked up that I am surprised I did not have a heart attack.

When the trekkers appeared in the distance I darted back into the jungle. In my present condition I might unwittingly tell the truth – a particularly unwise move when your pockets are stuffed with rupee notes of doubtful origin. Eventually the others passed, I rejoined the track and followed them placidly back to the camp.

That night I told my mother the true story, showing her the money in the belief that she would welcome this remarkable upturn in our family fortunes. But she backed away from me, her eyes wide with alarm as though I had presented her with a severed head. In hushed tones she ordered me to get rid of the loot immediately as the connection with the dead body had tainted it.

'Something bad happened in the jungle. We must not keep this money. You must give it back. Go now. Hurry. Quickly.'

I knew she was right. It had to be done for there were powerful forces out there which I did not understand.

After the light from the cooking fires had died down, I slipped out of the camp and hid the notes under the first bush I came across in the jungle. Then I held my palms together for a few moments as a sign of atonement, because it was unwise to be smug while standing alone in the pitch dark surrounded by swirling nats. Finally, with some relief, I said goodbye to the fabulous palaces and food-halls that were so nearly mine. But without telling Mum I kept a few notes in my pocket.

Before dawn next day the camp was up and by 7.30 the two groups were on their way up the winding track for the final assault on the high Pangsau pass. It would be a hard slog of thirteen miles through mountains to our next camp, but we were all fired up, for today we would cross the border into India.

Maisie and I walked together for most of the way, but sometimes I wandered off on my own, lost in my memories of this amazing adventure: the long line of trekkers and porters straining up the winding paths with such determination; glimpses of my hero, Georgie, on the back of a diminutive Naga, his ankles tied with string, a frown of pain on his face, then a sudden smile as he saw me.

Sometimes I saw my mother, like Cleopatra, gliding past and I would walk alongside her palanquin for a while, chatting to her.

'Are you all right, Steee?'

'No problems, Mum. I feel fine.'

'Where is Maisie?'

'No idea.'

'I said stay together. Go find her now. Don't get lost.'

'All right. I'm going.'

But I never did; not at once anyway. After all, this was my jungle. I could not get lost in it if I tried. I would deliberately sit down and daydream for a while, study an interesting insect, investigate a strange plant, or smell a flower, before jogging easily past all the porters and stragglers until I came up to Maisie.

'Where have you been? You had me worried.'

'Where do you think? I've been on the telephone.'

'Cheeky child.'

'Silly Boozie.'

These encounters may sound trivial, but they were not. They were a deliberate way of keeping an eye on my family. In the old days before Shingbwiyang we could trek as a regiment with Father in the lead and me as the 'tail-end Charlie'. But now we were individuals scattered in a large caravan – and I was responsible.

For several hours we trekked comfortably through open forest, but around midday we began to ascend a ridge. The incline became perilously steep, and although steps had been cut into the earth it was very tough going for the porters and the weaker refugees. Our progress slowed to a crawl and frequently stopped completely as someone lay down exhausted on the narrow track, unable to continue without help. It was like the Kumon range all over again. At last we reached the crest of a windswept ridge where a pyramid of loose rocks had been placed on the well-trodden grass. On top of the rocks was a human skull with BURMA scrawled on one side and INDIA on the other. This was the Pangsau pass. We were 4,000 feet high in the Patkoi Hills.

Well, my father, we made it. I wished you could have been with us to share that moment. But it was not to be.

I did not pause for more than a few minutes, nor did I look back. It all seemed so barren, even pointless, compared to the expectations of the thousands who had set out in May. Mum and George had not yet arrived but I found Maisie, and we set out together for the camp half-a-dozen miles away in India. I had no more tears to shed.

We rested the following day, dulled by a feeling of anticlimax. People mooned around the camp or lay under the tarpaulin, staring vacantly at nothing in particular. It was all rather strange. I moved cautiously through the fringe of jungle, for this was a foreign land: yet the food was the same, so were the people, the trees and the weather. It seemed all right so far but it could get worse.

I lay down next to my mother, cuddling up close, feeling safe and loved.

'Where are we going to in India, Mum?'

'I don't know, Stee.'

'Will we go to Louise's or perhaps Marie's?'

'I don't know.'

'Are they not in India?'

'Nobody knows, Stee.'

'What will happen to us then?'

'Stop asking these questions, Stee.'

I felt a lot worse after this. Clearly, since we knew nothing at all about the future, we were no better now than gypsies or vagabonds.

Once again we were on the trail at dawn to put in an eleven-mile trek by sundown, when we reached the camp at Nampong. Later that evening, word came that the sick and infirm were to be left here so they could receive adequate medical treatment. Those who could walk would proceed to the railhead where the others would eventually join them. It was a wise decision I suppose, because the non-stop trekking of the last few weeks had blighted the recovery of those like George who were seriously ill. But I did not like the idea of splitting up our family. However, Mum was adamant and although I argued with her she would not budge.

'You two must go,' she insisted. 'If you stay you will become sick, so go now. I will find you later Stee. Nothing will happen. Go.'

Reluctantly Maisie and I said goodbye to the others and set off at a blistering pace to the next camp, which was another eleven miles away. We had now reached the section of track built by the Indian Tea Association and General Stilwell's American Army, which was broad and firm with respectable gradients, quite unlike the Alpine ski slopes of the Kumon range that had bedevilled our Gurkhas' bulls.

I remember shuffling across a rickety cane and bamboo suspension bridge dangling over a river so clear you could see every detail under the surface. On the far side the bank gave way to an inviting shallow pool, and I gladly followed Reggie in for a dip. I was barely able to swim but I doggie-paddled happily close to the bank while Maisie looked on.

Before dawn the following day we cantered into the lead, racing along the delightful road that looped through the open forest. Signs of human activity were everywhere – stacked logs, lanes cut through the forest and copious tractor-marks, but no workers. At midday we emerged onto a small plateau, from which the path descended steeply to the bottom of the valley via one thousand steps. Each step was made from a log five feet long, pinned into the hillside and levelled on top with soil and gravel. We had arrived at the celebrated Golden Stairs, aptly renamed the Chocolate Staircase by those who had the misfortune to use it during the monsoon.

Apocryphal stories of the Chocolate Staircase had circulated among the refugees, spreading alarm and disbelief with each telling. To our weary minds, negotiating this obstacle eventually began to seem as problematic as going over Niagara Falls in a barrel or descending from the Eiffel Tower by umbrella. However, the staircase was entirely different during the wet and dry seasons. During the monsoons I could well imagine it as a dangerous and frightening avalanche of thick gooey mud. But today was dry and sunny and the Chocolate Staircase had once again become the Golden Stairs.

Maisie and I hopped down them, squealing with excitement. About half-way down we heard voices. Other human beings? Then we saw them, a dozen labourers, most likely from the road-building team, digging in the forest away to our right. Stone the crows! What a sight. We exploded with uncontrolled laughter and snatches of happy song.

'Hello. Hello.' Our voices rang out. 'We've walked from Burma. Yippee! The wicked witch is dead, yeah, the wicked witch is dead. We've made it. Hip-hooray. We beat the bloody Japs. Hooray!'

We waved and hooted with elation. They waved back, indicating that we should continue on down. Taking their cue, we stepped off the stairs and ran down the slope, slipping and sliding, happy, exuberant, free.

'We did it, Boozie. Come on.'

'Don't fall, Stevie. Wait for me. Hold my hand.'

Several yards of high-speed dry-slope skiing followed and we were down. Almost immediately my bare feet touched something warm and strange that made me shy away in alarm. When I glanced down I discovered we were standing on a road: a proper, level affair, free from thorns, rocks, deep pools and sinking sand. This was civilisation as I knew it. I did a quick jiggling dance on the smooth surface for the benefit of my poor feet, which had not known such bliss for five months.

Driven by the prospect of meeting more 'civilised' people we set off at speed along the level road, crossed another suspension bridge and were several miles further on when we heard the electrifying sound of a motor vehicle. I believe it partially deranged Maisie and me because we shouted and skipped for several minutes before running eagerly towards some figures in the distance. They waved back. Five minutes later we stood before them, keyed up and out of breath. With eyes that could barely take everything in we stared at them, anxious that they should not disappear like a mirage.

Four young men with fair crew-cut hair, jungle-green fatigues and muddy boots studied the emaciated girl and boy before them quizzically. Returning their stares were two brown, long-haired, dirty, bare-footed savages, the youngest of whom carried a curved cutlass in his right hand. I now know how ridiculous an aboriginal Australian must have felt when faced by Captain Cook in his immaculate naval uniform. I could not stop giggling.

Then the tall lanky man on the right, with three stripes on his shirt-sleeve, removed the cigar from his mouth. I cannot remember the precise words he uttered at this historic meeting. I think they were probably 'Hi there.'

'Great balls of fire!' I stood amazed. 'Yanks! Halleluiah.'

We swallowed hard and Maisie made a strangled noise.

'Haarr.'

I looked anxiously at her and realised she was having difficulty adjusting her eyes to so much accessible manhood.

'Gee! Where have you kids come from? Do you speak English. Parleyvoo? Er ... speak ... En ... gli ... sh?'

'Hello.' Maisie had found her voice at last, thank God. 'I'm Maisie and this is my little brother Stevie. We've walked from Burma.'

'Jeeesuss! D'yer hear that, Lou? Natives from up Jap country.'

I thought to myself, 'Oh shit, bloody cowboys,' but I held my peace.

'There's more of us just a little way back,' said Maisie demurely.

'Holy cow! More?'

She pointed to the Golden Stairs, down which a motley crowd of scarecrows were wobbling their way.

'Hey, look at that fellas. Wow-eee! Injuns! Get the Captain.'

I knew then and there I was not going to enjoy civilisation – but they had a jeep, and that made the difference. If we could get a lift, I would be polite.

Very soon there were people everywhere: laughing, crying, falling about and generally making a din, for on this day, 24 October 1942, the Great Trek of 421 miles had come to an end. There were not many of us. Those who were there were tired, sick and hungry. Torn scraps of clothing hung from undernourished bodies. But we had made it; we were the survivors; we were the ones who had braved the Valley of Death and reached safety.

Almost 50,000 people had set out to find sanctuary in India, yet fewer than half survived. Above all, I was conscious of their absence. I remembered their suffering and their lost hope. Yet they did not die in vain, for their light has never been extinguished in my mind. It is in their honour that I offer these inadequate words as a memorial, so that it cannot be said that they perished as though they had never been.

# Epilogue

My silver-handled kukri, which had been my constant companion for five months, was taken from me by the Indian authorities at the border town of Ledo. It was a clear indication that for me the war was over. My swag of rupee notes from the dead body could have been compromising, but I had the presence of mind to throw them down a latrine before I was searched, thus depriving the nats of their last laugh.

We spent several depressing weeks feeling disorientated and vulnerable in various refugee camps where we were sent to be fed, clothed and medicated. In early December we located my sister Janet and her husband, Warrant Officer Steve Peart, who were living in army married quarters at Jhansi, a two-day journey by train from Calcutta. Our reunion at their home was charged with emotion, for these were familiar faces we had thought we would never see again as we lay on our hessian sacks in the longhouse at Shingbwiyang.

Janet told us that Louise and her husband Warrant Officer Charlie Cross were in army married quarters a mere half-mile away. My eldest sister Marie, her husband Dennis Maule and her children were also safe and living in Simla. Later we received news that my half-sister Dorothy, her husband Captain Jack Hancock and all their children were safe, as was my half-sister Kate Brookes who had walked out through Tamu. Captain Rupert Brookes, my half-sister Queenie's husband, had also survived, but there was no news of Queenie or her daughter Joy.

And so our escape from Burma through the Valley of Death was over. The long journey of 3,000 miles, which began at Maymyo on 15 April 1942, ended at Jhansi on 13 December. During those eight months the elegant way of life we had enjoyed in pre-war Burma came to a dramatic end. It was never recreated. Our wealth was gone, our family scattered, and nothing could restore the spirit of those times. Also among the ashes were the remains of the once great British Empire, for which generations of my family had fought. For those who survived, the world would never be the same again.

Several years elapsed before I was able to piece together the confused story of what happened in Maymyo after we left. There is some evidence that Willie's wife Della, and her daughters Xelda and Gwen, tried to catch a train that was leaving for Myitkyina where, according to another source, Willie was waiting for them. Although the train was overloaded with refugees, a crowd of violent Chinese soldiers began fighting for space on it. It appears that Della was advised to return home as there was no hope of a safe journey to Myitkyina. Soon after her return to Lindfield the Japanese arrived and Queenie, Della and their children were taken prisoner. Ironically they were interned in King Thibaw's fort in Mandalay, close to where my father's Medical Supply Depot used to be.

During their detention Queenie's daughter Joy, a lovely girl just two or three years older than me, fell ill and died. My half-sister was so heartbroken that she pined away and died soon after. But Della and her daughters survived and were liberated by British forces when the Japanese slipped out of the fort through a secret underground passage on 20 March 1945.

None of the family ever lived in Maymyo again and I believe a hotel now stands where Lindfield used to be. But I often roam in spirit through the lost gardens and orchards of my childhood, and rest in the cherry trees where George and I first saw those strange iron flying birds that tried to kill us.

Mum, Maisie, George and I never recovered from the terror of our escape from Burma. Within a few months of our arrival in India a mental barrier seemed to have gone up in each of us which blocked out painful visions of the trek. In all the years that followed we were never able to summon up the courage to mention it again. Significantly it has only been the writing of this book that has prompted me to talk with Maisie about our escape and to speak to friends and relatives about it.

Soon after the war was over in 1945 my relatives, including Maisie, who had married a soldier in the British army, left India for England and Australia, while Mum, George, Marie and her family returned to Burma. I was left alone in India as a 15-year-old schoolboy at La Martinière

College, Lucknow. After finishing my studies I taught in a school in Malaya, and then spent a year in the oilfields in Borneo, before sailing for England in 1951. After that I never met any of my immediate family again, apart from Louise, briefly, in 1976 and, more recently, Maisie.

Mum eventually married an Anglo-Burmese man and found some peace of mind. She was with her own people again and her memories of India, the trek and her life at Lindfield slowly faded. George died when he was 42, and my mother two years after him in 1971.

By the accident of birth, I was privileged to be part of this story during the remarkable love affair between my parents. Although my material inheritance was only a torn shirt and threadbare shorts, I was bequeathed a spiritual inheritance beyond measure by Ma Sein and William Lindfield Brookes. I touch their feet in reverence and hold my palms together in their honour. They were as the Sun and Moon to me and I miss them still.

So all things passed, yet that hymn still whispers to me in the silence of the night:

> Time, like an ever-rolling stream,
> bears all its sons away;
> they fly forgotten, as a dream
> dies at the opening day.

May they rest in peace.

# *Acknowledgements*

I am indebted to my family and friends who steadfastly refused to let me walk away from the task of writing this book when my resolve faltered. Over a period of three years they put up with my neuroses, excuses and tears with the shrewdness of qualified psychotherapists. Chief amongst these was Maggie, my wife and anchor, without whose deep understanding and computer wizardry nothing would have been achieved. Our children Martin, Chris, Roger, Sarah and Tim sustained the family momentum, while our longstanding friends Dr Julius and Anita Lipner and Ute and Richard Sproulle prodded me at every meeting. My special tribute is accorded to Peter Hopkirk, who inspired me and was unfailingly generous with his advice and encouragement during the most difficult days.

I thank my sister Maisie, who played a vital part in my story, for permission to use her diary, photographs and letters; and my niece Patricia Cuzner for photos of my father.

Finally my thanks go to my editors Gail Pirkis and Hazel Wood who undertook the unenviable task of shaping my manuscript.

Stephen Brookes
Cambridge
1999